# MY PRETEND FRIEND

## JO NAUGHTON

Grosvenor House
Publishing Limited

This book is published by
Grosvenor House Publishing Ltd
Link House
140 The Broadway, Tolworth, Surrey, KT6 7HT.
www.grosvenorhousepublishing.co.uk

A CIP record for this book
is available from the British Library

ISBN 978-1-83975-154-7

Some names and details have been changed to protect the
identity of the people whose stories are included in this book.
Bible references are from the New King James Version unless
otherwise stated. The Message and TPT are also used
to help reveal the heart of certain passages

*This book is dedicated to every precious person who is brave enough to face the truth for the sake of their future. It's not always easy, but truth is the path to transformation.*

# Acknowledgements

Mum:
Thank you for modeling a life of love and gratitude, and for never showing a trace of self-pity, even in bereavement.

My husband, Paul:
Thank you for speaking the truth and for being God's tool of transformation in my life.

Rita Field:
Thank you for your love and unswerving support in life and ministry.

Tim Collins:
Thank you for investing your wisdom, time and talents in this book.

Freisa Davila:
Thank you for lending your creative genius to this book and this ministry.

Ruth, Robert and Wendy:
Thank you for investing hours of your time in painstaking proofreading.

# Contents

1. Meet Your Pretend Friend    1

**PART ONE : THE CULPRITS**

2. Difficulty    13

3. Agony    26

4. Injustice    45

**PART TWO : ITS WEAPONS**

5. Thoughts    69

6. Lies    90

7. Isolation    102

**PART THREE : GOD'S REMEDIES**

8. Healing    114

9. Perspective    125

10. Praise    136

# Chapter 1

# MEET YOUR PRETEND FRIEND

You have an inner enemy. It wants to prolong your pain and trap you in a dark place. It creates feelings of injustice and steals your joy. Worst of all, it seeks to stifle your life. Self-pity is vicious. However, it is also a master of deceit and pretends to be your friend. It reminds you of all the reasons why you should stay sad. It strokes your wounds, but does not heal them. It tells you that no one understands your suffering. It may counsel you to keep others at arm's length. Alternatively, it could push you to share your sad story with anyone who will listen. It always digs a hole and invites you to climb inside.

A few years ago, I was flying to the Middle East to be the main speaker at a big women's conference. There was a slight problem: I had completely lost my voice. I don't mean that it was a little scratchy. There was nothing, nada! It had been that way for five long days and the doctor told me that it would take between two and three weeks for my voice to return to normal. God promised that I would preach so I was confident that He would come through (even though it was nerve-racking!) As I was praying mid-flight, I realized that I had been unwell four times in just four months. "That's not right," I mused. So I asked God, "If all is well, then why am I getting sick so often?" (I encourage you to be an enquirer. When you see patterns or issues that you know aren't God's plans, ask the Lord to reveal any underlying causes. You will be amazed what you will learn.)

Almost instantly, the Lord revealed the problem by holding up a mirror of my behavior. I would be gearing up for a ministry trip then I would feel some flu-like symptoms. "Oh no, that's not fair! Why me?" I would moan to myself. "I cannot believe this is happening again to me. I pray over my health and yet here I am fighting another fever." I would feel badly let down. Then I would think, "Oh well, it's time for Jo the hero to step up once more. Even with aches and pains, I will crack on as I always do. I will minister anyway." By that time, I would probably be writing a text to our head of prayer sharing my plight. Instead of arising myself, I would ask for the intercessors to arise. Let me explain it simply. Sickness would knock at my door. Self-pity would open it wide and pride would say, "Come on in."

## MY PROBLEM

I was getting sick too often because my first response to life's little ups and downs was self-pity. God has given you and me a shield of faith which we need to hold up when the enemy throws his fiery darts (Ephesians 6:16). Unwanted symptoms should have prompted me to fight back with my faith. Instead of listening to self-pity's lies, I should have reminded myself of the promises of God over my health. I can't afford to feel sorry for myself whenever my journey through life takes a tricky turn. And I can't afford to see myself as some sort of superhero simply for carrying on.

Lying whispers in my ears were causing me to feel sorry for myself when I should have been following Scripture's instructions: "And the prayer offered in faith will make the sick person well..." (James 5:15 NIV). Faith changes things, so we don't want to crowd it out with heart issues. Proverbs 23:23 says, "Buy the truth, and do not sell it..." It suggests that truth comes at a price. That is because the truth can be painful. It is easier to believe that someone else is the problem. However, we are sometimes responsible for our own issues, or at least I am! God was essentially telling me that self-pity was the problem.

With tears trickling down my checks, I told God how sorry I was. Did I mention that I was on a plane sitting beside a random stranger? I sure was glad that my hair was long enough to cover my tear-stained face! I repented of self-pity and dealt with my pride. I then asked God to cleanse my heart and heal my body. When I landed that evening, although I was still silent, I knew that the root problems had been dealt with. I whispered my way through the following day, but my heart was at peace. I woke up on the morning of the conference in my hotel room. I was due to preach in about three hours. I opened my mouth. After a week of silence, a booming voice emerged. I was healed, but I was also changed.

Self-pity has many guises. It is a mindset that believes, "My lot in life is rough." Although we may project positivity publicly, we are often down. Self-pity is also a filter. We view our lives through grey glasses. We expect setbacks. When things go wrong or people let us down, we regard it as typical. By contrast, we may see the circumstances of others through rose-colored spectacles. Self-pity is a spin doctor. It puts a negative spin on our lives. Finally, self-pity is a place we can go to alone and replay our problems. It can be a weirdly comforting 'friend'.

# A POWERFUL PROBLEM

We all struggle with self-pity in one way or another. Sometimes we don't realize that we are being weakened by its influence. On other occasions, we are aware that we are feeling sorry for ourselves, but we think it is justified so we surrender. What's more, because it sounds bad, most of us would prefer to deny that it is a problem. As a result, this powerful inner enemy does much of its work beneath the radar. It is a bigger issue than most of us realize and it often succeeds in putting a lid on our lives. You may wonder how such a seemingly harmless thing could hold you back so much. Here are five reasons why it is a particularly powerful enemy.

# 1. WHAT DO YOU EXPECT?

Self-pity negatively programs our thinking. It makes us pessimistic. We anticipate problems and presume we will be disappointed. It causes us to expect delays and difficulties. Proverbs 23:18 (KJV) explains that your "... expectation shall not be cut off." Put simply, this verse means that we get what we expect. In the light of this scripture, think about the impact self-pity can have on anyone who listens to its lies. Simply by expecting failure, we could be delaying our breakthrough. Every time we predict difficulty, we could be opening the door to problems. Imagine what a huge influence self-pity could be having on your life right now.

Our faith is vital to progress in every area of life. Mark 9:23 tells us that, "... all things are possible to him who believes." If I have faith, I can move the mountains in my life and it is my faith that pleases God. Faith is therefore vital. Hebrews 11:1 explains the manufacturing process of faith: "Now faith is the substance of things hoped for..." This verse explains that faith is the result of hope. Just as ice is made from water so faith is made out of hope. You cannot make ice unless you have water and you cannot develop faith without hope in your heart. In contrast, when you are full of hope, your faith will grow. This means that both hope and faith are vital to our success.

So what is hope? It is not wishful thinking, as the world suggests. Hope is confident expectation based on what the Bible promises. Hope is full of optimism. It is when we expect good things because we know that God is good. We need great expectation in order to grow faith in our hearts. Unfortunately, it is almost impossible to be full of hope while we are feeling badly done by. Self-pity chokes hope and extinguishes the faith you need to transform your situation. It pretends to be your friend, but it is deceptive.

# 2. ALL EYES ON ME

Self-pity is inward-looking. It has self at the center. It dwells on personal problems and wallows in difficulties. It focuses on the unfairness of *my* life. It magnifies *my* problems (and often unwittingly minimizes the goodness of God). When we feel sorry for ourselves, we become consumed by our own issues. Other people's struggles seem insignificant by comparison. When self-pity sets in, our concern for others wanes. As a result, we neglect their needs. If this is a big issue for you, know that self-pity is almost always rooted in low self-worth and it is driven by pain. The more you are healed, the easier it will become to break free from this enemy.

Whenever 'self' is at the center, life is hard work. The enemy tempts us to focus on the unholy trinity of me, myself and I. Generosity feels good and is energizing. In contrast, selfishness is never satisfied. Feeling sorry for ourselves sucks the life out of us. Philippians 2:3 (NLT) says, "Don't be selfish... Be humble, thinking of others as better than yourselves." I love how the Passion version of the Bible translates verse 4 of the same chapter: "Abandon every display of selfishness. Possess a greater concern for what matters to others instead of your own interests." Any time I am feeling sorry for myself, I am focusing on my lot in life rather than on the needs of others. According to these verses, I am outside God's will.

Scripture tells stories about the mistakes and suffering of others so that we can grow. Queen Vashti is featured at the start of the book of Esther. She was married to an extremely powerful man, King Ahasuerus. The king decided to throw a huge party for the men in his kingdom - both the nobility and the commoner. At the same time, Queen Vashti hosted many of the women. After about a week of partying, the king sent a team to bring his queen to the men's quarters. He wanted to show off her beauty. We don't know why Vashti refused. Maybe she felt belittled. Perhaps she was just having a good time with the girls and didn't want to break up her party. Either way, Vashti was thinking about Vashti rather than honoring her husband. It must have felt great to refuse the king. I imagine that her guests might have enjoyed the unusual spectacle. Perhaps the ladies all cheered or burst into fits of giggles after the king's men left. Self-centeredness always feels right at the time, but it is never beneficial. King Ahasuerus felt slighted and Vashti was stepped down from her position. Selfishness demoted her from queen to commoner in just twenty-four hours.

# 3. PROLONGING PAIN

Self-pity draws out the healing process and prolongs your pain. It makes your road to restoration so much harder. Let me explain. Your journey to wholeness will probably be made up of a series of supernatural encounters. Each time God brings you back to an old memory and you pour out your pain, He will heal another precious piece of your heart. In between each encounter, life will of course throw its curveballs. You will go through difficulties and disappointments just like anyone else. However, self-pity will have something cynical to say each step of the way. It will try to erode your faith. You will hear an inner voice telling you lies like: "And I thought I was healing", "Nothing ever works out for me", or: "Why do I bother? I'm back where I started." It aims to keep you bound by pain. It is important when we are wounded that we pour out our pain in God's presence. Self-pity wants us to rehearse our hurts rather than release them.

Self-pity will try to tell you that none of your healing really happened in the first place. You will be in danger of doubting your progress and giving up. Faith is foundational to healing. Whether your body or your heart needs a touch from God, it is vital that you keep your eyes on the Lord every step of the way. Self-pity shifts our focus from God's infinite ability and onto our bleak circumstances. It opens the door to doubt and this can severely slow down your journey to wholeness. It is often the reason why we go round the same old mountain, dealing with the same old issues time and again.

# 4. WORD POWER

Proverbs 18:21 tells us that death and life are in the power of the tongue. Our words can breathe life and they can also wreak havoc. Mark 11:23 teaches that we receive - not only what we pray but what we say. That makes perfect sense because we are made in the image of God. He spoke and light appeared. He created the sun, the moon and the stars with His words. Hebrews 11:3 says: "... the worlds were framed by the word of God." In the same way, we frame our worlds with our words. If you start speaking what self-pity is saying, you may unwittingly dismantle the wonderful work that the Lord is doing.

When life is painful or difficult, faith reminds you that God always makes a way where there seems to be no way. It rehearses the Lord's faithfulness. This lifts your spirits. In contrast, self-pity tries to make you tell yourself that you cannot cope with any more pain. The truth is that we all talk to ourselves! Maybe some people do it more often than others, but we all speak to ourselves sometimes. Self-pity will try to make you despair. "Nothing ever works out for me!" You may say out loud: "I can't handle this pain anymore!", or: "It's never going to happen", or: "I'm a total failure!" Just as we must watch what we say to other people, we cannot afford to speak negatively to ourselves. If I am saying that nothing ever works out for me, I'm cursing my own progress.

## 5. NO ENTRY

There is one more reason why self-pity is harmful: it makes us ungrateful. It is impossible to have a thankful heart while we are feeling sorry for ourselves. This is a serious spiritual problem. 1 Thessalonians 5:18 says, "In everything give thanks; for this is the will of God in Christ Jesus for you." If I am out of the will of God for my life, by definition, I am in disobedience. Not only that, Psalms 100:4 in the Message explains how to get into God's presence: "Enter with the password: Thank you!" Thanksgiving is the way into the presence of the Lord. Self-pity denies us sweet fellowship with the Holy Spirit. His presence is breath to our souls. Times of refreshing come from the presence of the Lord. See Acts 3:19. Without His breath, life itself is dry.

Let's set out on this journey with two things in mind. Firstly, self-pity tries to worm its way into all our lives. For some, this may be an obvious problem. For others, this could be a subtle issue. However, I have no doubt that it is a universal enemy. Secondly, self-pity is serious. We must not see it as a trivial matter. It wants to steal your promises, kill your joy and destroy - or at least delay - your destiny. Please join me on a journey to expose it and then evict it from our hearts and lives. Let's pray.

**Heavenly Father,**

I don't want to give self-pity any place in my life. I ask You to shine your light into the depths of my heart and reveal any habits that keep me bound and weigh me down. As I read this book, show me any place where I have fallen prey to self-pity and help me to kick it out of my life. I want to be full of faith and expectation so that I can fulfill my highest potential. Please speak to me Spirit of Truth as I read and take me on a journey to freedom and fulfillment.

In Jesus' name, I pray,

Amen.

# Part One

# THE CULPRITS

Life is tough. We experience soul-destroying disappointments and get hurt along the way. We get betrayed and rejected. We lose people we love. We get let down and forgotten. Self-pity can be ushered into our lives by a whole host of painful circumstances. Let's look at some of the most common culprits.

# Chapter 2

# DIFFICULTY

We all go through hard times. Perhaps you have been pursuing your promotion for far too long. You know that you were made for more than the life you are living. When you look around, you feel shortchanged. You may have been fighting over your finances for years. You are faithful in tithing, but still struggle to make ends meet. Perhaps your marriage has been a painful mix of heartache and letdowns. You dreamed of the fairytale, yet you woke up to the reality of unfulfilled promises or loneliness.

You may say that your entire life has been a catalog of disappointments. You could be fighting for the restoration of your family, battling debt, held back in ministry, or struggling with serious health issues. The truth is that:"... man is born to trouble..." (Job 5:7). The word for trouble in the Hebrew is âmâl and it means sorrow, pain, stress and strain. Trials are part of life and battles are inevitable. That does not stop them from being awful, but what makes them almost unbearable is when our pretend friend self-pity elbows its way into the picture.

## BUMPS

The Lord called me to bring our ministry from the United Kingdom to the United States. That may sound easy, but I assure you there were challenges. The UK is a tiny island about around 5,000 miles away from America - and I hardly knew anyone there. When God gives us dreams, He doesn't disclose how difficult the road to fulfilment will be. We would probably never start if we knew the struggle that was in store for us! Maybe you have been pursuing goals for years and you are bewildered by slow progress. When times are tough, it is easy to feel sorry for ourselves. At this point, our pretend friend is usually not far away.

In early 2019, the battle to bring Healed for Life to the United States intensified. Just when I was certain we were about to come into momentum, progress seemed to grind to a halt. It was about a month before one of our events and bookings were few and far between. The conference center and accommodation were confirmed, contracts were signed but no one seemed to be registering. My team and I were praying and believing for bookings. One morning, when I checked numbers, the stark reality hit me like a punch in the guts. "This is awful. Why is no one booking?" I asked myself. "What am I doing wrong? God, why aren't you coming through? This is a disaster."

I felt like I had stepped out in obedience and God had not bothered to come through. I knew we would get there in the end because the world needs this ministry, but I felt dejected on the way. The more I thought about the low numbers, the deeper I sank. I sat for an hour and despaired over the situation. I did not tell anyone what I was going through because I knew it was my battle to fight, and in any case, I needed my team to stay in faith. For about two weeks, I felt myself slipping towards depression.

God always comes through, of course. The places filled up and the Holy Spirit moved in life-changing power at the event. Every person was touched to the core by the healing love of the Lord.

Nonetheless, I returned home emotionally and physically exhausted. I knew I needed to look back at the month leading up to our conference. As I prayed, everything became clear: I had allowed self-pity to camp in my heart. Nearly every negative thought was about me. I was upset that I had stuck my neck out, that I had worked so hard and that I might look stupid. It was all about me. I was not feeling desperate because the multitudes would have to wait a little longer for their healing. I was upset because I wanted my breakthrough. Self-pity drove out my joy, quenched my faith and almost led me into depression. I was stunned. It was around that time that I realized I needed to write a book on the subject! Self-pity had sneaked in and I had entertained it.

## WHAT DOES GOD SAY?

Feeling sorry for ourselves when life is difficult is understandable, but it is dangerous. Remember that faith is of the heart. Romans 10:10 says, "For with the heart one believes..." Faith does not develop in our heads, it lives in our hearts. If my heart is full of self-pity then there will not be the room or the right atmosphere for faith to rise up and fight my battles. The kind of faith that moves mountains in our lives grows deep inside. When our hearts host negativity, it can paralyze our faith.

The first passage I ever learned by heart was James 1:2-4 (NIV): "Consider it pure joy, my brothers and sisters, whenever you face trials of many kinds, because you know that the testing of your faith produces perseverance. Let perseverance finish its work so that you may be mature and complete, not lacking anything." Did you hear that? The Bible tells us to be joyful when life is hard! Why do you think that is? We know from Nehemiah 8:10 that joy releases strength - and we need to be strong when life is tough. When we feel sorry for ourselves in the middle of testing times, our spirits are low and our energy is depleted. Our pretend friend wears us down. Daniel 7:25 (AMPC) highlights one of the devil's end-time strategies against the church. It says he "shall wear out the saints of the Most High..." Self-pity is one of the trusted weapons satan uses to wear us down.

## EXHAUSTED

There is a reason why God instituted a day off each week. We need regular rest in order to be our best. Exhaustion can be debilitating. One of the greatest victories of Prophet Elijah's life is told in the first book of Kings. After three years of drought, Elijah came out of hiding to confront the false prophets of Baal in a showdown of power. The prophet gathered the nation of Israel and created a contest between Baal and God to prove His Lordship. After the prophets of Baal tried desperately but unsuccessfully to call down fire from heaven, it was Elijah's turn.

First, he repaired the broken altar. This would have involved pushing massive boulders into place. Then he carried twelve rocks to the altar. That alone would have been quite a workout but his day's labor was only just beginning. Elijah dug a deep trench around the altar. He collected a load of wood and placed it on top. Then he hacked a bull into pieces. Think about the effort required to chop up a huge animal! After placing the bull pieces on the altar, he asked helpers to pour four barrels of water over the mound. Elijah then began to pray and God answered by fire! The entire sacrifice was consumed with flames. Immediately after the extraordinary display of God's power, Elijah personally slaughtered 450 Baal worshippers. After that, Elijah entered a period of intercession, then ran supernaturally quickly to the capital city before the heavens opened and rainfall ended three and a half years of drought.

## BREAKING POINT

Elijah had a grueling few days. He must have been physically and emotionally exhausted. This strong prophet of God wore himself out. When we are weary, our defenses are down. Challenges that we would usually overcome fairly easily can seem insurmountable. Elijah had spent a good part of his life contending with a wicked woman called Jezebel. Although she was a powerful enemy, the prophet knew that his God was greater. However, with his energy spent, Elijah was intimidated by Jezebel's threats. One day, he was winning mighty victories and calling fire down from heaven. On the next, overwhelmed with exhaustion, Elijah ran away from Jezebel.

1 Kings 19:4 (NLT) says: 'Then he went on alone into the wilderness, traveling all day. He sat down under a solitary broom tree and prayed that he might die. I have had enough, Lord," he said. "Take my life, for I am no better than my ancestors who have already died."' After winning an array of brutal battles, our warrior gave up and wanted to die. You can hear self-pity taking root in his heart. His focus was no longer on saving his beloved nation. His attention was not on the might or faithfulness of God. He felt dejected.

## NO ONE UNDERSTANDS ME

Remember that self-pity pretends to be our friend. It tells us that no one else understands our situation and it tries to convince us that we are right to be downbeat. It makes doom and gloom seem appropriate - and weirdly comforting. Elijah must have felt justified in his despondency. He had given his all to the ministry and yet his worst enemy was still standing while he was broken. He ran from everything that was bothering him and sat alone and nursed his wounds. He was fed up, lacked faith and lost the will to fight.

Despite this despondency, God met Elijah at his point of need. The Lord sent an angel to minister to his servant, providing food, water and even supernatural strength. The prophet could have encouraged himself in the Lord like King David did when he lost everything at Ziklag (see 1 Samuel 30). Elijah could have burst out in praise to God for His faithfulness. He could have arisen once again in faith with fresh encouragement and energy. But the prophet dwelt on the injustice of his situation. He used his newfound energy to run to a cave and hide.

## GOD, I'M IN THE PIT!

Once again, the Lord reached out to his beloved servant and met with him in the cave. He revealed His power and His precious presence to the prophet. Sadly, Elijah seemed to be unchanged by this extraordinary encounter. How do I know that? God asked the prophet the exact same question twice. Once before manifesting Himself to his servant and once afterwards. "What are you doing here?" God would not ask the same question twice unless He was hoping for a different answer.

Self-pity skews our view of everything. Two people could be sitting in the same meeting when the word of God is preached. Both might be facing terrible trials. One could be encouraged and refreshed while the other could be left untouched. One could be grateful for a life-changing message, while the other might be thinking, *"You don't know what I'm going through. I can't risk believing because I don't want to get disappointed again."* Our responses to the opportunities that come our way often determine their impact in our lives. Self-pity explains why lifelines are likely to fail. It disregards help. It even sees blessings through a grey filter. It can cause us to turn in on ourselves.

## THE THIEF

Self-pity stole a great deal from Elijah. Let's look at his situation from a different perspective. He could have been celebrating his conquests. Fire literally came down from heaven and consumed a sacrifice soaked in water. What a phenomenal victory! The people of Israel concluded that Baal was a false god and they promised to serve the Most High. What an incredible harvest of precious souls! A three and a half year drought that had disabled life in Israel ended with a game-changing downpour. What a wonderful answer to prayer. I believe that this could have been Elijah's finest hour.

Instead, the prophet was overcome with anguish. The joy of the Lord is our strength so we need to guard our joy, especially when we are weary. Drained of all joy, he was weaker than ever. Self-pity also undermined his belief in God. The prophet's powerful victory a few days earlier should have fueled his faith for another remarkable conquest. However, he took His eyes off the Lord of the breakthrough. Instead, he was fixated by Jezebel and her threats. This was not his finest hour. It was probably his most disappointing defeat. Why? He listened to the lies of self-pity and gave in to its counsel.

## IT SHOWS

Our responses to pain and pressure are a good way of assessing the condition of our hearts. They reveal whether self-pity is a factor in our lives. God asked Elijah why he was hiding in a cave. His answer is revealing: "I have zealously served the Lord God Almighty. But the people of Israel have broken their covenant with you, torn down your altars, and killed every one of your prophets. I am the only one left, and now they are trying to kill me, too." 1 Kings 19:14 (NLT).

He started by describing how loyal he was to the Lord. That was true, but his eyes were on himself. He was not making this statement by faith to invoke even more of the favor of God. I think there was probably a sense of injustice in his voice as he asserted, "I have zealously served..." He then explained how awful everyone else was. He was not standing in the gap on behalf of his nation. He was bemoaning their backsliding.

Elijah then informed God that he was the only true prophet left and that everyone was trying to kill him. One of the top tricks of self-pity is to try to convince us that we are the only ones going through difficult situations. Elijah believed the lie that he was abandoned. Unfortunately, his feelings clouded his judgment. One of his last statements was not true and the other should not have been a problem. Many God-fearing people were still alive and a mere mortal was seeking his life. Elijah was tending his wounds by believing all was lost and it was all about him.

Self-pity often defies logic. Jezebel said that she wanted to kill Elijah so he ran away and told God he wanted to die. If he really wanted it all to end, he could have just let Jezebel have her way! Whenever we stop making sense, we need to examine our hearts. Elijah ran to a cave: a dark, lonely place. You might not have a physical place where you go to hide, but perhaps you have an emotional den to which you retreat when life gets too much.

## PAUL'S CAVE

My husband Paul has always been a positive, faith-filled man of God. But any time he grew really weary, he used to slip into self-pity. He was so good at it! God called him as a young man to start a church in London. Paul started with just three helpers: two old Irish ladies and a middle-aged man. They began meeting in a home, but within four weeks they had grown enough to rent a small hall. Every Sunday, Paul arrived at the venue at the crack of dawn. He swept and mopped the floors, unblocked and cleaned the toilets, moved the furniture, put out the chairs and then set up the sound system. He led worship, hosted the service, took up the offering, preached, prayed and then dismissed the people. Afterwards, he dismantled the equipment, stacked the chairs, put away the pulpit and locked up the building - with only occasional help from others.

Whenever he grew really weary, one of his first responses was self-pity. It would not take much to trigger his silent tantrums. When people who promised to help let him down, it could easily tip him over the edge. "Nobody cares," he would recite inside. "It's not fair. I'm doing all this alone and for what?" Driving home, he would rehearse all the reasons why his life was so difficult. He would retreat to an invisible cave. A cave is a secret place. It is not the secret place of the Most High where we meet God (see Psalm 91:1). It is the secret place where we go to dwell on all the reasons why our lives are hard.

Paul wouldn't give up because he knew God had called him. He was obedient - but he was not always willing. Isaiah 1:19 provides heaven's success formula: "If you are willing *and* obedient, you shall eat the good of the land." Obedience is about what we do. Willingness is about *how* we do it. Eating the good of the land speaks of fulfilment in life. Sometimes, Paul's heart was right. All too often, he would gripe and grumble while he followed the Lord's instructions. Remember: "... the Lord does not see as man sees; for man looks at the outward appearance, but the Lord looks at the heart." (1 Samuel 16:7). Obedience is the first step towards pleasing God. However, the right heart is the deal-breaker that opens doors. Although the church grew, Paul would often retreat to his imaginary cave to complain. Self-pity was producing attitudes that were holding back the blessing of God - not only over Paul's life, but probably the whole church too.

There were times when Paul felt that the whole world was on top of him for weeks on end and no one was on his side. It was not just church that provoked self-pity. If friends cancelled plans to see him, he felt sorry for himself. If money was tight, he felt wronged. If I messed up, he felt I was against him too! One day he was reading a book about how the enemy seeks to oppress believers. He looked up at me and said, "God just told me that I suffer from self-pity." "At last!" I shouted. "It has dogged you for as long as I've known you and crippled you on numerous occasions." That very moment, he vowed to the Lord that he would not allow it to nest in his life any longer. He went to God in prayer and repented. He chose to shut the door on behavioral patterns that had hounded him for years. No more shutting down or blaming everyone else. No more sulking when times were tough. He took an axe to his imaginary cave and smashed it to pieces. The change was amazing. He has been a happier, stronger and more resilient man ever since.

## ELIJAH'S END

It was while Elijah was nursing his wounds in the cave that God called time on this mighty man of God and raised up Elisha in his place. We don't know for certain that his destiny was cut short, but I think it is fair to assume that was the case. A conversation between God and the prophet resulted in the immediate promotion of his servant. Self-pity always seeks to take us out of the purposes of God. If this enemy can take out a general like Elijah, then we too need to be on our guard.

Paul the apostle was whipped, beaten with rods, stoned, shipwrecked and imprisoned. He was deprived of sleep, food and water. He lived without basic comforts. Nevertheless, he showed amazing resilience. By keeping mission-minded, he seemed to save himself from self-pity. He wasn't focused on fulfilling *his* dreams. He was determined to accomplish God's purpose. Of course, we would hope that our dreams *are* God's purposes! A slight shift in emphasis means we can endure suffering and set-backs without being distressed. When we live to serve Christ no matter what the cost or discomfort, it will help to deliver us from self-pity.

I love the story that the brilliant Welsh pastor Wynne Lewis used to tell. Soon after Pastor Wynne took over the leadership of a growing church in London, a man would stand up in service after service and cry out: "Woe is me for I am undone!" After a few weeks, the pastor got fed up. The next time the fellow repeated his mantra for all to hear, Wynne retorted from the pulpit in his wonderful Welsh accent: "Well do yourself up, boyo!" We have to fight self-pity like we would battle any other spiritual enemy. It is tempting to drown in our own sad circumstances. However, it only ever keeps us from rising up in faith and victory.

## MISTAKES

It is all too easy to assume that really spiritual people don't stumble - that somehow they never make mistakes. That is simply not true. The Bible says that the righteous *do* fall, up to seven times a day! The devil loves to use our mess-ups to make us lay down our weapons. The enemy wants you to see your failings as disqualifications. He wants you to bemoan your blunders as though they take you out of the race. You need to remember that everyone makes mistakes. What makes the righteous different is that they get back up afterwards. The Lord wants us to have faith in the power of the blood of Jesus to wipe away our errors. When we take our eyes off ourselves and our shortcomings and instead look to God, He gives us the strength to stand again.

Ephesians 2:8 in the Amplified reminds us of the way things are in the Kingdom: "For it is by free grace (God's unmerited favor) that you are saved (delivered from judgment and made partakers of Christ's salvation) through [your] faith. And this [salvation] is not of yourselves [of your own doing, it came not through your own striving], but it is the gift of God." The Lord does not call the qualified. He qualifies the called. Your works did not save you and they cannot absolve you, but the blood of Jesus can. Don't let self-pity tell you that you cannot continue. "Though the righteous fall seven times, they rise again..." (Proverbs 24:16). Anytime you fall, just get back up. Be a cat, not a pig!

# THE POWER OF HOPE

When we choose, like Abraham, to hope against hope, we will find the strength to arise from discouragement. Self-pity opposes three of the most important attributes that we need to nurture: hope, faith and thanksgiving. It is almost impossible to be hopeful and down in the dumps. It is extremely hard to be strong in faith while feeling sorry for ourselves. And we cannot be filled with both gratitude *and* self-pity. Let's ask the Lord to forgive us for harboring wrong attitudes and let's start the process of changing our perspective. Let's pray:

**Heavenly Father,**

I have been through many difficulties. Sometimes, it has felt like life is too much. (*Now tell the Lord which hard times have hurt you the most. Share in as much detail as possible why life has felt so difficult.*) I have been worn down by battles and have been exhausted at times. I ask You to heal me of the hurts along the way. I now realize that the devil would like to use the trials of my life to keep me bound by self-pity - to delay or derail my destiny. I am so sorry for allowing myself to be dragged down. Thank You that You always provide a way out in every situation. You are always good to me and I am grateful. Help me to always see Your protection in the midst. Help me to change my attitude towards the bumps in the road so that I may come out the other side stronger than ever.

In Jesus' name, I pray,

Amen.

# Chapter 3

# AGONY

Our first child suddenly died at the age of 2. Naomi was our joy. She had just reached the age when she would giggle at life's little surprises. Naomi loved music and could happily sing along to her favorite nursery rhyme for four hours straight! "Head and shoulders, knees and toes, knees and toes..." she would shout as the music played. Our little girl had blonde curly hair, bright blue eyes and a magnetic personality. After a weekend fighting a cold, Naomi seemed to get better. Then she went rapidly downhill. She was rushed to hospital, but within 24 hours of arriving at the emergency room, our baby had passed away. Meningitis was her vicious killer.

Naomi's sudden death shattered our lives. I did not know my heart could feel such agony until that time. Mornings were awful. For a few short moments after waking up, I would forget what had happened. Then reality would hit me like a punch in the guts. Silent tears are sometimes the saddest. All too often, they hide a debilitating ache beneath the surface. If the truth be known, I never really imagined that I could be fully restored. However, we serve a God who can heal us anywhere we hurt. He does not put a bandaid on inner agony. Psalms 147:3 (AMPC) is clear: "He heals the brokenhearted and binds up their wounds [curing their pains and their sorrows]." He is a master restorer.

# YOUR HEALER

If you have been broken by the loss of someone you dearly loved, please know that God is able to take *all* your pain away. Isaiah 61:1 says that Jesus was sent to heal the broken-hearted. Take that verse personally. Your Lord was sent by your Father to fully restore every corner of your heart. We have a chapter on healing in part three of this book. Getting healed of heartache is not a one-time event. It is a journey of encounters in the precious presence of God. At our two day Healed for Life conferences, we have seen countless people supernaturally restored after experiencing terrible pain. Even as you start to recover, keep going back to the Lord for another touch of His healing love any time sad memories surface.

During the weeks and months after our daughter died, God brought genuine healing to my husband and me. Our Heavenly Father reached into the depths of our innermost beings and He pulled pain out. By the first anniversary of our daughter's death, we were well on our way to wholeness. Within a couple of years, all the sadness was gone. He completely restored our souls. We were also blessed with two more truly wonderful children.

# DEFINED BY TRAGEDY

Although my heart was healed, tragedy had defined me. I saw myself as a survivor: someone who had been to hell and back and made it out alive. When I stood at the school gates waiting for my son to finish lessons, I viewed myself as the bereaved mum. Others had normal stories (or so I supposed), but I had lost my little girl. I was always aware of which people knew about our tragic loss versus those who did not know. It was my ever-present issue. It was my elephant in the room.

It was not just that our first child died. Although our son was perfectly healthy, our second daughter suffered a great deal. Abby was born with her umbilical cord wrapped twice around her neck. Every time I pushed during labor, she was being suffocated. By the time she was born, our baby had been starved of oxygen for ten minutes and had no detectable heartbeat. I remember calling to my husband, "Go with the baby!" The crash team who had been called to the scene rushed with the little one to intensive care. After the doors closed, I was left alone in the birthing room with one midwife.

"Did I have a boy or a girl?" I asked, but in the heat of the emergency the midwife had not checked the gender of the child. It was thirty minutes later that I was told I had had a little girl, but that she was fighting for her life. Abby spent the first ten days of her life in intensive care. Within two days of getting home from hospital, other problems emerged and she was readmitted. Our daughter endured about fifteen operations by the time she was six. Painful medical procedures became a normal part of her life and she faced daily challenges. I did not just see myself as a grief-stricken parent. I was a victim mother with two difficult stories.

## MARKED BY SCARS

It is one thing to have a scar where there was once a wound. It is another thing to see that scar as a mark that sets you apart - even after the pain has been taken away. There are many life-altering events that can brand our lives. Tragedy is just one. You may have been marked by abuse, abandonment, disease, divorce, poverty or any other painful experience. God's desire is that we are branded by His love, not our misery. Song of Songs 2:4 (AMPC) says, "He brought me to the banqueting house, and his banner over me was love [for love waved as a protecting and comforting banner over my head when I was near him]." This paints a picture of God's plan. He wants His love to be the identifying mark over our lives.

Although I was healed, my identity had been branded by tragedy. Proverbs 23:7 says, "As a man thinks in his heart, so is he..." Any time our identity is rooted in pain, it is a problem. It will affect our thoughts and influence our decisions. Ultimately, it will guide the direction of our lives.

# THE WORST

When we go through life-shattering circumstances, it is easy for us to believe that our pain is worse than the hurts of others. We are overly aware of our inner turmoil and assume that everyone else is better off. Our view of our suffering sets us apart in our own hearts. Sometimes, our nearest and dearest unwittingly fuel these feelings with their constant concern. Believing that our war wounds are the worst can negatively affect our attitude and our behavior. We may feel more deserving of sympathy or attention. When we don't get it, we dive even deeper into self-pity.

If I believe I have been through more pain than others, I will also think that I am different. When we see ourselves as different, we make allowances for all sorts of things. We accept isolation and allow negative thinking. When we believe our lives are unusual, we may think that we cannot achieve the breakthroughs that others enjoy. We feel as though we are watching everyone else live their lives on the other side of a glass screen. This perspective does not create an atmosphere for faith or determination. It makes us feel like giving up. According to scripture, it is also a lie.

Ecclesiastes 1:9 says, "That which has been is what will be, That which is done is what will be done, And there is nothing new under the sun." The New Living Translation puts it this way: "History merely repeats itself. It has all been done before. Nothing under the sun is truly new." The Bible clearly teaches that each one of us is unique. God has a tailored plan for your life that reflects your individual design. At the same time, one of the core lessons of Ecclesiastes is that nothing we go through is new.

## SEEN IT ALL BEFORE

History regularly repeats itself. Countless couples across the world have lost their children to untimely death. Indeed, many have lost entire families. Scores of parents have suffered like me and come out strong. Others have endured battles that are similar to yours and emerged successfully on the other side. Every test or trial has been faced by others down through the centuries. "The temptations in your life are no different from what others experience..." 1 Corinthians 10:13 (New Living Translation).

The Greek word for temptation here is the same as the one for trial. What you and I have experienced has been endured by many others the world over. When we realize that our struggle is not all that different from the battles that others have had to fight, it can help us to put our lives into some sort of perspective. If we take our eyes off our individual issues and instead look to the greatness of God, the Lord can start to work within. We will deal with this important issue in greater detail in our chapter on perspective in part three.

## ENTITLED

My suffering also made me believe that I deserved extra compassion from the people around me. When times were tough, I expected special concessions. When I was behaving badly, I thought I should be absolved of any guilt. After all, I was a bereaved mother. When life was good, I saw myself as a hero for being happy. I felt entitled to special treatment. I believed I should be handled differently. This even affected my relationship with the Lord. I expected God to answer my prayers because He owed me a consolation prize. In Matthew 17:20b, Jesus said, "If you have faith... you will say to this mountain, 'Move from here to there,' and it will move; and nothing will be impossible for you." Scripture is clear. Faith, not self-pity, moves mountains.

I don't know what you have gone through. Perhaps you have been betrayed by people you trusted with your very life. Maybe you have lost someone very special. You could have been thrown away by the love of your life. You may have suffered soul-destroying heartache. Although I don't know your story, I do know that satan seeks to persuade you that your struggles have set you apart. It is almost like you hear whispering in your ear convincing you that your suffering separates you from other people.

## HAND OVER YOUR INNER IMAGE

One day, God in His mercy ministered to me in a life-changing encounter. I saw myself standing before the Lord with two toddlers in my arms (my girls) and one child at my feet (my boy). I sensed God tell me to take Naomi - our child who died - into my arms and give her a big hug. I did so. Then, in my mind's eye, I handed her into the arms of my Heavenly Father. I gave her to Him. Next, in my mind's eye, I held my daughter Abby in my arms. I gave her a tight cuddle and then I transferred her into God's hands. Finally, I picked up my little boy, Benjy. I embraced him and then placed him into the Lord's care.

After I entrusted my children to the Lord, I sensed Him asking me to surrender my identity as a victim mother. I had never before acknowledged that my inner image was tainted by victimhood, but it was true. For far too long, I had seen myself as a battle-weary mom. I struggled to be grateful for the goodness of God because hardship dominated my view of my life like a huge mountain filling a landscape.

When God spoke, I knew it was time to act. Just as you would remove a coat, I took off that telltale victim-mom uniform that I had worn for years and laid it down. I relinquished my tainted identity. In that moment, I knew who I was. Far from being a disadvantaged mother, I realized that I was a dearly loved daughter of the Most High. I no longer clung to my old inner image. I felt fulfilled just from knowing that I was favored by my Heavenly Father. Something changed in my outlook after that encounter. I surrendered my excuses and I stopped wanting sympathy.

Sometimes self-pity may feel like your only real friend. After all, it encourages you to wallow in melancholy and nurse your wounds. In a perverse way, feeling sorry for ourselves can feel great. The moment you make a decision to kick it out of your life, you will realize that it was in fact a traitor to your true nature - something that sought your demise. You and I cannot enter a new season while we are feeling cheated by our last season. Self-pity traps people in the pain and gloom of the past. Why not take a moment now to write down all the experiences you are going to bring to the Lord for Him to heal? You can deal with them in chapter 8.

## CHEERLEADERS

When we think of the great cloud of witnesses cheering us on (Hebrews 12:1), we normally imagine that they are encouraging us to accomplish great things in God's kingdom. But what if they are just as focused on showing support when we go through storms? Many of them suffered terribly. Adam and Eve went through the tragedy of seeing their firstborn murder their other son. The pain and conflict must have been unbearable. Noah witnessed a global crisis brought on by human depravity. Judah suffered awful loss: his wife and two sons died prematurely. Joseph was beaten up by his brothers, sold as a slave and sent to prison for a crime he did not commit. David was rejected or betrayed by nearly everyone he trusted. Despite such tragedy, each of these heroes went on to fulfil their destiny.

Esther's parents died when she was a child so she was raised by her cousin in a foreign land. It would have been all too easy for her to give up on life. But this young woman would not allow her suffering to keep her inward-looking. She would not allow her difficult upbringing to keep her from rising high. She would not allow self-pity to keep her down. Instead, she faithfully followed every instruction of her cousin and was eventually crowned queen in a foreign land. I won't describe the appalling persecution that the apostles suffered after Jesus died and rose again. These men and women suffered terribly. Yet they accomplished so much that helped so many.

Those who went before us understand pain, but they are examples of how to overcome a crisis. We can allow our suffering to define us, or we can determine that we will come out the other side healed and strong. 1 Corinthians 10:13 reminds us that there is always a way out: "No temptation has overtaken you except such as is common to man; but God is faithful, who will not allow you to be tempted beyond what you are able, but with the temptation will also make the way of escape, that you may be able to bear it." We discovered earlier in this chapter that the word for temptation also means test. No matter how hard the trial or tragedy, God promises us that there is a way out.

## ROTTEN LOT IN LIFE

Helen's parents were desperate to have a baby boy. When a girl was born, they were gutted. They didn't have a name for a daughter so the baby was nameless for weeks. From as early as she can remember, Helen felt rejected. At just three years of age,

Helen's mom turned to liquor and became an alcoholic. She would work and drink, hardly ever getting involved in her child's life. The only time that Helen saw her dad was during silent, awkward dinners when he ignored his daughter. They were a wealthy family who lived in a poor neighborhood. Their home was robbed regularly so Helen lived in fear.

"Growing up was awful," Helen explained. "I went to a school where I was the only black child. The girls in my class despised me and told me I stank. I had no friends. White people rejected me because I was black. Black people rejected me because my family was wealthy. I didn't belong anywhere. I was trapped in a prison of loneliness. Then when I was eight, the sexual abuse began. Every month when my uncle visited, he molested me. I dreaded his visits and felt stained by the violation. I was desperate for it to stop, but he told me that if I spoke to anyone about it, he would hurt me badly. I was terrified and felt powerless."

## I'LL DO IT MY WAY...

As soon as she was old enough, Helen left home to start a new life. She was determined to shake off her childhood and make something of herself. Ever since she was young, Helen had wanted to be a nurse so she put all her energy into getting into this as a career. But instead of new opportunities, Helen was met by repeated rejections. "I started to think that there was something wrong with me," she explained. "Everything I touched turned to garbage. I felt like a complete failure and wanted to give up." It was at this time in her life that Helen first attended one of our healing conferences.

Right from the start, God began to do a deep work. "The Holy Spirit brought buried memories to the surface and then healed my heart - again and again and again. It was so liberating. Then when the issue of self-pity was mentioned, I realized that this was the story of my life. I had to make a choice to accept responsibility for wrong thoughts and feelings. I realized that I had been accommodating this awful enemy and so I decided to kick it out. It was like something snapped inside. I realized that I was loved and accepted by my Heavenly Father just the way I was. Most of all, I realized that I was not a victim. I had victory. For the first time, I felt free. I was free to make my own choices, free to be grateful, free to enjoy my life."

Helen stayed on her healing journey and attended several of our conferences. A few years later, she applied one more time to nursing college and was accepted. She graduated with a first class degree, secured an excellent job and has since been promoted several times. Although she is still on her healing journey, she keeps a guard around her heart to make sure that self-pity cannot pull her down anymore.

# IS GOD AGAINST ME?

The book of Ruth starts with the story of Naomi. Ruth 1:1-5 (NLT) sets the scene: "In the days when the judges ruled in Israel, a severe famine came upon the land. So a man from Bethlehem in Judah left his home and went to live in the country of Moab, taking his wife and two sons with him. The man's name was Elimelech, and his wife was Naomi... And when they reached Moab, they settled there. Then Elimelech died, and Naomi was left with her two sons. The two sons married Moabite women... But about ten years later, both... died. This left Naomi alone, without her two sons or her husband." What a tragic story. Naomi left home with her precious family, but returned without them. Only Ruth, her daughter-in-law, was by her side.

Tragedy marked Naomi. When she got back to Bethlehem, everyone was pleased to see her. Ruth 1:19-21 tells the story of her return: 'So the two of them continued on their journey. When they came to Bethlehem, the entire town was excited by their arrival. "Is it really Naomi?" the women asked. "Don't call me Naomi," she responded. "Instead, call me Mara, for the Almighty has made life very bitter for me. I went away full, but the Lord has brought me home empty. Why call me Naomi when the Lord has caused me to suffer and the Almighty has sent such tragedy upon me?"'

When we don't get healed, our pain can cause unimaginable anguish. In Hebrew, the literal meaning of Naomi is 'my delight'. This woman did not want people to use her name because she had been marked by loss. Instead, she wanted to be called Mara, which means bitter. She was hurt and angry. When self-pity grips our hearts, it is all too easy to blame others for our suffering. It was Elimelech (Naomi's husband) who took the family to Moab, not God. And at a time in history when everyone knew the importance of names and the power of words, they called their sons Mahlon (meaning sick) and Chilion (which means pining). No one knows why these three men died, but one thing is clear. God was not responsible for their deaths.

Naomi told the people of Bethlehem that she went out full but came back empty. Self-pity always magnifies pain while minimizing any good in our lives. Naomi had not returned empty. She had an extraordinary daughter-in-law with her. Ruth loved Naomi and was loyal, almost to a fault. She left her homeland in order to remain with her mother-in-law, but self-pity could not see this blessing in the midst of tragedy. This young woman that Naomi overlooked ultimately became God's channel of redemption.

## ANGRY AT GOD

Naomi was upset and angry. The difficulty with this is that the only one who can heal you of your pain is the Lord. If you have been holding Him responsible for your agony, I encourage you to lay this burden down. He is good and everything He does is good. James 1:17 (AMPC) says, "Every good gift and every perfect (free, large, full) gift is from above; it comes down from the Father of all [that gives] light, in [the shining of] Whom there can be no variation [rising or setting] or shadow cast by His turning [as in an eclipse]." There is not even a hint of evil or darkness in God. I know it feels powerful to hold anger, but it actually drains your strength.

Seeking specific answers is different. The Lord never minds when we ask Him what is going on in our lives. It is normal to feel confused! Asking 'why' is often part of the healing process. Even Jesus cried out to His Father from the cross, saying, "My God, My God, Why have you forsaken Me?" (Matthew 27:46). You can hear the desperation in those words. Jesus was heartbroken and felt forsaken by His Heavenly Father, but He still knew God and so was assured that He is good. Before we go any further, if you have been angry with God, would you allow me the honor of leading you in a liberating prayer?

**Heavenly Father,**

I have believed the lies of the enemy that You were to blame for my pain. I am so sorry. I realize now that I was wrong. You are good and You are a good father to me. Please forgive me for blaming You. I don't understand why I had to suffer the way I have. It has been heartbreaking and I have hurt in places I didn't know existed. I am sorry I blamed You when in reality, You are the only one who can help. Forgive me, I pray, and I ask instead that You would start to heal my heart.

In Jesus' name, I pray,

Amen.

# THE MAN WITH MANY PLANS

There is a well-known verse in Jeremiah 29:11 (NLT) which says, "'For I know the plans I have for you," says the Lord. "They are plans for good and not for disaster, to give you a future and a hope."' There are two important points about God here. Firstly, He has plans. There is not just one master plan. If life throws curveballs, He is able to reroute our lives with new plans. Secondly, His plan B (or C, or D) is always good. The plans He has are for your good - to give you a great future. Sometimes heartbreaking things happen. However, God always has a plan for your restoration and He even ensures there is retribution or compensation. God heals our hearts, brings blessings into our lives (as well as the lives of others) and He makes sure that the devil regrets harming His people! He has many ways of doing this. I have experienced God's ability to work things together for good, over and over again.

After Naomi and her daughter-in-law returned to Bethlehem, God revealed His plan for restoration. Ruth married a very special man called Boaz and the newlyweds had a son called Obed. Ruth 4:14-16 (NLT) says, 'Then the women of the town said to Naomi, "Praise the Lord, who has now provided a redeemer for your family! May this child be famous in Israel. May he restore your youth and care for you in your old age. For he is the son of your daughter-in-law who loves you and has been better to you than seven sons!" Naomi took the baby and cuddled him to her breast. And she cared for him as if he were her own.' This baby boy eventually became King David's grandfather and he is named in the lineage of Jesus Christ! When we are ready to lay down the arguments that go with self-pity, we are positioning ourselves to see the redeeming goodness of God in our lives.

# PLEASE DON'T GO

My US spiritual mom called me from hospital one Saturday afternoon. We had a wonderful conversation and she told me one last time how much she loved me. Prophet Cathy Lechner was probably the most affirming human being I have ever had the privilege of knowing. She loved so lavishly that at first, I found it a little overwhelming! Eventually, her affections broke down my barriers and I learned how to better care for others just by receiving from her. Prophet Cathy was a remarkable lady.

She sounded strong when she called, but she was very unwell. In less than 24 hours, Cathy was rushed into ICU. She passed away a week later. This precious woman of God left behind seven sensational children. In addition, her untimely death shocked thousands around the world who had been touched and transformed by her ministry. Matthew 7 tells us that torrential rains, overwhelming floods and roaring winds hit us all. The wise and the foolish alike are unexpectedly thrust into times of difficulty and tragedy. Although forecasters can warn us about impending hurricanes or tornadoes, we do not always get a sign that personal turmoil is on the horizon. Let's go back again to Job 5:7 which says that: "...man is born to trouble." Trouble means sorrow, stress and strain.

We all experience turmoil. The death of a loved one can shatter whole families and even communities. An unexpected job loss can strip us of our dignity and security. Serious illness can shake even the strongest of souls. There are countless causes of sorrow. The fact that storms are inevitable does not stop them from being painful. And that is not all. The enemy wants to use the crises of life to crush God's precious people. I want you to know that you can come out the other side of even the most tragic situations.

# FINDING THE WAY OUT

Jesus told a story in Matthew 7 that shows us how to protect our hearts and lives when storms strike. The Lord described the rain, wind and floods engulfing two houses. It is very easy in the midst of trauma to give up praying and put down our Bibles. Matthew 7:24 in the Passion Translation says, "Everyone who hears my teaching and applies it to his life can be compared to a wise man who built his house on an unshakable foundation." It is the doing of the Word of God in any and every situation that makes us strong. The wise man does what Jesus says, even *during* the storm.

In the same story, Jesus likens us to fools if we don't put the Word to work in our lives: "But everyone who hears my teaching and does not apply it to his life can be compared to a foolish man who built his house on sand." (Matthew 7:26 TPT). The story explains the outcome when we give up during tough times: "When it rained and rained and the flood came, with wind and waves beating upon his house, it collapsed and was swept away." Matthew 7:27 (PTP). If we give up doing the Word when it gets tough, there is a danger that everything will fall down around us.

When Prophet Cathy went to be with the Lord, my heart was broken. Every time I pictured her face, the pain intensified. Tears just kept falling. The evening she died, my son sent me a recording of his first ever preaching. As I listened to him share the Word of God, I felt so proud of him. All of a sudden, I cried out, "I want to tell my mama!" (You see, I always shared my children's milestones with my American spiritual mother who prayed daily for them both). I fell to the floor and wept. Pain from the deep recesses of my soul streamed out as I cried before the Lord.

I wept hard and loud before God. I told Him exactly what was hurting me in that moment. After some time, my tears slowed down and I went to bed. The following morning I realized that I didn't hurt the way I did the day before. God had started healing me. My heart still hurt, but not as badly as before. Five days later, I was in Maryland in the US ready to run one of our Healed for Life conferences. I went for a walk early in the morning. As I worshipped, more pain surfaced so I shared my sadness with the Holy Spirit (also known as the Comforter). I wept - gently this time - for about an hour as I walked and talked with the Lord. This encounter was not as dramatic as the first one, but it was just as healing. It is important to seek healing any time pain arises.

# HEAVEN'S INSTRUCTIONS

Lamentations 2:19 says, "Pour out your heart like water before the face of the Lord". If the storm has hurt you, you need to be healed. Your heart was not made to contain pain. When the Lord created you in His image, he designed your heart for the giving and receiving of love. He formed your heart for fellowship. When we bury pain, we push it into corners of our hearts that were meant to be filled with love. Ecclesiastes 11:10 says, "Remove sorrow from your heart."

Notice that these two verses from Lamentations and Ecclesiastes are instructions not invitations. We are *doing* the Word (like the wise man who built his house on the rock) when we get in His presence and ask Him to heal our hearts. We are being obedient when we pour out our pain in prayer. Storms often come unexpectedly. The sudden onslaught can leave us feeling battered and bruised. That is why it is vital that we are healed. I am going to dig deep into the subject of how to be healed in part three.

Pouring out your pain is not the same as surrendering to sadness. We must not allow forlorn thoughts to dominate, that will only pull us downhill. Maybe there have been times that you have felt yourself slipping into despondency. Why wouldn't you if you had suffered terribly? Of course, we must pour out our pain in prayer as we have already said. That is not the same as giving in to the heaviness that tries to fill our souls. When you are suffering, listen to your thoughts with extra attention. Are they all true and in line with God's word? Are they all helpful?

The week that Prophet Cathy died, I remember crying out to God, "I'm not ready for this. I'm not ready to lose my mentor!" The following day, I went back to the Lord and corrected myself. "Father, thank you that I am ready for every season." Changing my thoughts dispelled the sense of being overwhelmed. Of course I was still broken-hearted, but I was not despairing. I needed to be healed, but I was full of hope. We can choose, even in the midst of tragedy, to align our thoughts and comments with God's word.

# WHAT ARE *YOU* SAYING?

You probably know the verse that says, "Let the weak say I am strong." (Joel 3:10) It is amazing how much we can encourage ourselves by speaking faith in the middle of difficulty. I am not talking about denying hurt or pushing down pain. That is neither healthy nor godly. Yet we can choose what we say and how we talk - even in tough times.

The hardest thing I ever did was give birth to my son. A baby's head usually lengthens to help it pass through the birth canal. Not my boy's. He was a gentle giant with a whopping head. It seems funny now, but when I was in labor, I worried that I would never get him out. My girls slipped through in a matter of moments. It was seriously hard giving birth to my son and I was feeling defeated. In the midst of pain and pressure, determination arose and I cried out, "I can do all things through Christ who strengthens me!" Benjy was born. I have no doubt that my words paved the way for his arrival.

Even in the midst of the storm, we can choose what comes out of our mouths. We can push past the pain and declare vengeance. We can overcome feelings of being overwhelmed and proclaim new strength. We can seize the moment and force some sort of victory in the middle of a tragedy. When you are weak, choose to use your tongue to strengthen yourself. Say: "This may be tough, but I'm coming out stronger than I went in," or: "God has brought me through before and He will do it again." Even: "I can handle this because God is with me and He will never leave me."

We can also choose what we do. Please don't ever throw down your weapons. You need them all the more during times of tragedy and suffering. Matthew 7:24 says that the wise man does what Jesus says. We need to do what He says when the winds are howling just as we do when the sun is shining. During the storm, we need to pray. During the storm, we need to speak the word. During the storm, we need to do the things that will help us come out strong.

**Heavenly Father,**

Please forgive me for the times when I have allowed self-pity into my heart. I don't want to be defined by tragedy so I give you any victim mentality that I have been holding onto. I ask You to forgive me for thinking my lot in life was worse than the lives of others. I realize now that there is nothing new under the sun. Others have suffered trials like mine and have come out strong. Thank You that this will be my testimony too.

Thank You that even in the midst of agony, I do not need to despair. You have my life in Your hands and I will come out of this season. Even when I walk through the darkest valley, I will not be afraid, for you are close beside me (Psalms 23:4 NLT). You will bring me out stronger than when I went in. Even in the middle of pain, help me to filter negativity out of my thoughts and to focus on the truth. Help me to say the things that will build my life.

Thank You that You are my healer, You are my deliverer, You are my strong tower. You are my ever-present help in times of trouble. I love You and I trust You.

In Jesus' name, I pray,

Amen.

# Chapter 4

# INJUSTICE

Naomi was limp when she arrived at hospital by ambulance. After being ushered into an assessment area, blood tests were carried out. She was then transferred to a ward. Our little girl lacked any vitality. Four hours later, test results confirmed what was obvious to the eye: Naomi was very sick. There is a measure used by medics to assess infection levels in the blood. It is called a CRP. For a two year old, a CRP of 15 or more should be treated with antibiotics. Naomi's blood test results arrived at four o'clock in the afternoon. Her CRP was 236 so she needed antibiotics urgently.

To our utter dismay, the doctor looking after our little girl would not give our daughter medication until a urine sample had been obtained. Despite evidence of overwhelming infection in her blood, the doctor decided she wanted to 'rule out a urine infection' before treating Naomi. Our baby had not drunk for a long time so she was not passing anything. Five long hours passed. Eventually, I could not stand waiting any longer. I grabbed an aluminum dish, laid it beside my little girl's legs and pressed down on her bladder area. I somehow managed to squeeze sufficient urine into the dish which I delivered to the doctor. "Now, please give my daughter antibiotics," I pleaded. By this time, it was nine thirty in the evening. Naomi was given an injection - but it was too late.

# TOO LITTLE TOO LATE

An hour later, our little girl had a seizure which lasted forty five minutes. The medics managed to stop the fit, but Naomi was soon struggling to breathe. She was rushed into a treatment room and then had the first of three cardiac arrests. Despite fighting all night to save her life, by seven thirty the following morning, our precious princess had passed away. She was two years old.

A medical review of the case confirmed that if Naomi had been given antibiotics when she arrived at hospital (or even when blood results came through in the afternoon), she would almost certainly have survived. Our little girl would have had a future. We were dealing with the loss of our adorable child, but also with the knowledge that she died as a result of medical negligence. Of all the doctors on duty at the hospital that day, Naomi was treated by the one pediatrician who was not thinking. It was wrong. It was unfair. I felt like life itself owed us an apology. I could not understand why this had happened to our little girl. What did our daughter do to deserve such substandard care? Why was her life cut short?

# DON'T TRY TO MAKE THINGS BETTER

Around the time that Jesus was born, King Herod ordered the execution of all Jewish baby boys in Bethlehem who were aged two and under. The entire town must have been filled with grief. One particular woman is mentioned in Matthew 2:18 (NLT): "A cry was heard in Ramah—weeping and great mourning. Rachel weeps for her children, refusing to be comforted, for they are dead." This grieving mother was devastated, but rejected any reassurance because there was nothing that anyone could do that would change things. Perhaps you could put it like this: she wanted either her son back or nothing. That's certainly how I felt during a dark season.

When terrible things happen, we can feel justified in clinging to our pain. The fact that we were wronged can make us want to nurse rather than heal our wounds. Negligence, betrayal, abuse and injustice can make us hold on to the view that we are victims. According to this mindset, a victim is set apart by their circumstances. A victim must be pitied. A victim deserves special concessions. We cannot imagine that anyone could understand. At the same time, we look at the lives of others through rose-colored spectacles and assume that their trials are less testing than ours. Being wronged can easily fuel feelings of self-pity. Don't take the bait.

## WHEN WE DON'T GET WHAT WE DESERVE

King Saul hired David as a harp player when he was a teenager. 1 Samuel 16:22 (NLT) shows how impressed the king was with the young musician: 'Then Saul sent word to Jesse asking, "Please let David remain in my service, for I am very pleased with him."' David continued to work hard for his boss and spiritual father: "So David went out wherever Saul sent him, and behaved wisely. And Saul set him over the men of war, and he was accepted in the sight of all the people and also in the sight of Saul's servants." (1 Samuel 18:5). David worked hard, kept a loyal heart and always did what he was asked. When we give our best to people we expect things to go well. I'm sure David assumed that this was the beginning of the greatest season of his life.

Unfortunately, King Saul unexpectedly became envious of his spiritual son's success. If we rely on people's praises to build us up, then we will feel insufficient when nothing is said. Saul craved the celebration of the people so when they started to cheer louder for David, he became jealous. David did nothing wrong and yet went from rising star to mortal foe as a result of one random song sung by a group of ladies. The story is told in 1

Samuel 18:7-9: 'So the women sang as they danced, and said: "Saul has slain his thousands, and David his ten thousands." Then Saul was very angry, and the saying displeased him; and he said, "They have ascribed to David ten thousands, and to me they have ascribed only thousands. Now what more can he have but the kingdom?" So Saul eyed David from that day forward.'

# IT'S NOT RIGHT

Imagine the situation. David was the celebrated spiritual son of King Saul and he served him with a loyal heart. He was living in the palace at the king's request and was best friends with Prince Jonathan. David loved the Lord with all of his heart and only wanted to do what was right in His sight. I am sure he was glorifying God as he watched the prophetic word over his life start to come to pass. It seemed as though he was poised for further promotion. Instead, one silly song turned King Saul (and his entire army) against the shepherd boy. One day, David was enjoying plush accommodation and royal portions. The next, he was forced to flee for his life and begin living rough.

It was wrong. David did nothing to deserve such treatment. Yet on a daily basis, he was hounded by soldiers as though he was a fugitive. He hid from the authorities in woods and caves. You can hear how much it was hurting him in Psalms 4:2 (NLT): "How long will you people ruin my reputation? How long will you make groundless accusations? How long will you continue your lies?" The injustice of the situation was paining David but it also fueled feelings of self-pity. Listen to David's attitude in Psalms 69:20 (NLT): "Their insults have broken my heart, and I am in despair. If only one person would show some pity; if only one would turn and comfort me."

Self-pity led David into anger and offense. He spent the next six verses dwelling on his outrage. It didn't help him and it never helps us. The turning point in this psalm came when David took his eyes off himself and those who had offended him and instead looked to the Lord. In Psalm 69:29, David was in a mess and so he asked for heavenly help: "But I am poor and sorrowful; Let Your salvation, O God, set me up on high." After he asked for help, he changed his tune. It is as though he now knew what he needed to do. David stopped complaining and instead gave God praise: "I will praise the name of God with a song, And will magnify Him with thanksgiving." (Psalms 69:30). Praise is one sure way to drive out self-pity and to clear our hearts of clutter so that faith can arise inside. This psalm became a prophetic template of the suffering, death, burial and resurrection of Jesus.

# NOT AGAIN!

Isaac was Abraham's miracle son. He was one of three famous fathers mentioned throughout the Old Testament. The Lord even called Himself "The God of Abraham, Isaac and Jacob". But for a season in Isaac's life, most of his time was spent digging wells! He had been asked to leave the country where he was living so he was trying to find a new home for himself and his people. In order to put roots down somewhere, he needed a well so that his family could be assured of drinking water. He quickly found the wells that his dad Abraham had dug so he must have restored them with great joy.

A huge amount of hard work paid off and they soon had water. However, local farmers would not allow Isaac to keep a well that he had dug and they claimed it as their own. All that effort was for nothing. It would have been easy for Isaac to feel sorry for himself. The injustice of having the fruits of his labor taken away must have been awful. But Isaac would not allow himself to be deterred. He started digging another well. Once again, he put his heart and soul into his efforts and his labor paid off. Well number two was restored. However, it must have felt like Groundhog Day because the exact same thing happened again. Imagine the frustration he must have felt. It was not right. The local people were exploiting his hard work. I am sure the enemy tried to make Isaac give up.

Perhaps you are in that position. You have prayed and obeyed, but every time breakthrough is in sight, something goes wrong. Satan wants you to sink into self-pity. The enemy wants you to give up. Galatians 6:9 (AMPC) teaches us an important lesson: "And let us not lose heart and grow weary and faint in acting nobly and doing right, for in due time and at the appointed season we shall reap, if we do not loosen and relax our courage and faint." Please don't let the discouraging lies of the enemy make you walk away from the plans that God has for you. This verse is clear: you will be rewarded if you don't give up.

Isaac would not give up and instead went back to digging. Genesis 26:22 reveals the rewards for perseverance even in the midst of injustice: 'And he moved from there and dug another well, and they did not quarrel over it. So he called its name Rehoboth, because he said, "For now the Lord has made room for us, and we shall be fruitful in the land."' The enemy uses self-pity to try to get us to put down our weapons. He knows that when we won't give up, we will see the promises of God for our lives come to pass.

## THIS CAN'T BE HAPPENING AGAIN

As I shared in the previous chapter, eighteen months after our son Benjy was born, I was back in the labor ward having another child. Everything was going well until the final stages of delivery. The clinician in charge suddenly changed her tone: "Call the crash team! The cord is wrapped twice around the baby's neck." Every time I had pushed, my baby had been choked. It soon became clear that our little one had been starved of oxygen for ten minutes. They got the baby out and then ran off. My husband went with the medics and they rushed to neonatal intensive care.

I was left alone in the birthing room with just one nurse. "Did I have a boy or a girl?" I asked in a daze. The nurse had not noticed in the midst of the emergency. Thirty minutes later, I was told that I had given birth to a little girl, but that she was fighting for her life. The nurse wheeled me into a side room where they proceeded to stitch me up. Suddenly a cry came from deep down inside, "What is it with me and baby girls?"

There is something about facing pain again that can stir self-pity. It is bad enough when it happens once. Twice seems terribly unjust. Maybe you have gone round the same old mountain too many times. Our pretend friend will try to get you rehearsing all the reasons why it is so wrong. The problem is that these arguments never help. When we are battling the same giants over and over again, we need to find the strength to make a stand.

Thank God our little girl was born on a Sunday morning. My husband texted every pastor he knew so thousands of saints were standing in the gap. After a night in labor and the shock of the delivery, I did not have the strength to wage war. However, there is always something we can do. As I lay on that hospital bed, I declared, "I don't know right now if my little girl will live or die, but Lord, I promise You this: the devil will regret attacking us. I will pray more and I will win souls as vengeance." When I look back at that day, I am grateful to God for the opportunity to make a stand - even when I did not know how things would turn out.

# A LIFE OF INJUSTICE

Joseph deserved a medal for enduring injustice! He was betrayed by his brothers for money and sold into slavery. Even though he was a dearly loved son, he had to work like a dog as a servant. Things did not get better. While he was serving faithfully, he was falsely accused of rape by his boss's wife. I cannot imagine how terrible that must have felt. He resisted the temptation of having an affair with this woman. His reward? He was tried and convicted of being a violent criminal. Joseph was sent to prison. While he was inside, he was in physical as well as psychological agony. Psalms 105:18 (AMPC) describes his torment: "His feet they hurt with fetters; he was laid in chains of iron and his soul entered into the iron."

He was suffering because of the wickedness and lies of others. Thirteen years of Joseph's life were taken from him. He should have been enjoying his prime, but instead he was in captivity. Maybe that's your story. You have been betrayed and mistreated and missed out on much of your life as a result of the actions of others. I know that the enemy will try to keep you bound with the sense of injustice. When something is wrong, anger can easily build inside. It can even reach a boiling point. Rage does not make us powerful. It does not punish perpetrators. All it does is wind us up and drain our strength. It adds insult to our existing injury.

## TICKET TO FREEDOM

When I read the story of Joseph's life, I see no sign that he ever sank into self-pity. Perhaps it happened for a season, but he must have lifted himself out of it. If he had been feeling sorry for himself, he would not have noticed the sad faces of the butler and baker. He had to take his eyes off himself to obtain his ticket to freedom. Genesis 40:5-7 (NLT) says, 'While they were in prison, Pharaoh's cup-bearer and baker each had a dream one night, and each dream had its own meaning. When Joseph saw them the next morning, he noticed that they both looked upset. "Why do you look so worried today?" he asked them.'

These men did not come looking for Joseph. It was Joseph who noticed their anguish. Not only that. He cared enough to ask them what was wrong. Our pretend friend encourages us to keep our eyes on our own issues. And even if we do see the pain of others, it tells us that we already have enough of our own problems. Joseph refused to dwell on his dire situation. As a result, the butler and baker both shared their troubling dreams with Joseph and he gave them the interpretations. Self-absorption is a trap that keeps you imprisoned.

Genesis 40:20-22 (NLT) explains what happened next: "Pharaoh's birthday came three days later, and he prepared a banquet for all his officials and staff. He summoned his chief cup-bearer and chief baker to join the other officials. He then restored the chief cup-bearer to his former position, so he could again hand Pharaoh his cup. But Pharaoh impaled the chief baker, just as Joseph had predicted when he interpreted his dream." God gave Joseph an opportunity. It came by opening a door called consideration.

## FORGOTTEN

Then our hero faced another hurdle. After everything Joseph did for the butler, he forgot his promise to tell Pharaoh about Joseph's plight. I don't mean that it slipped his mind for a few days. Genesis 40:23 - 41:1 (NLT) says, "Pharaoh's chief cup-bearer, however, forgot all about Joseph, never giving him another thought." For days and even weeks after the butler was restored, Joseph must have woken up each morning thinking, "Today is the day! The cup bearer will remember me today!" However, that never happened. Imagine how upset he might have felt! Two full years passed. Do you know the difference between a year and a full year? I think a full year is when it feels like forever. Genesis 41:1 (NLT) says, "Two full years later, Pharaoh dreamed..."

How many times do we look at the delays and disappointments of our lives and feel forgotten? If the enemy can keep us thinking that we have been forsaken, he can trap us in our misery. We think we have been short-changed. In truth, this kind of mindset is evidence that we have become self-absorbed. Although the great patriarch Job had every right to feel dejected, it never helped him. He not only felt sorry for himself, he also hankered after the sympathy of others: "Have pity on me, have pity on me, O you my friends, for the hand of God has struck me!" Job 19:21. Sometimes we just want people to acknowledge the cruelty of our lives. It was only when Job took his eyes off his terrible troubles and instead reminded himself of the genuine goodness and greatness of God that his circumstances started to change.

Imagine if Joseph had protected his heart against self-pity until that point and then given in at the end. Being forgotten is horrible. It creates a sense of rejection and often fuels feelings of injustice. With no human way out of his situation, Joseph somehow managed to maintain a forgiving heart. I believe it was this that God was observing. Proverbs 4:23 (NLT) says, "Guard your heart for it determines the course of your life." The Lord must have been watching and waiting for the moment that Joseph was ready for his destiny. Despite terrible suffering and great injustice, he kept his heart humble.

The butler eventually remembered Joseph and told Pharaoh about the man in jail who could interpret dreams. God won't tolerate unforgiveness. He is merciful and expects it of us too. I wonder what would have happened if Joseph had harbored resentment against the cup-bearer? God was the one in charge, so perhaps it would have delayed his departure from prison. Thanks to the butler's tip off, Joseph was summoned to appear before the king to explain the meaning of his dreams. As a result of the clarity of Joseph's interpretation and his wisdom, Pharaoh told him, "I hereby put you in charge of the entire land of Egypt." (Genesis 41:41 NLT). It is always worth keeping our hearts right, even in the face of terrible injustice. Self-absorption and a sense of entitlement are arch enemies of victory.

# ROBBED

Self-pity nearly killed Jonah. He resented the Lord showing mercy towards the people of Nineveh. Their undeserved blessing somehow made him feel robbed. Does that sound familiar? He was grieved when he witnessed God showing favor to unworthy sinners. He could not handle the kindness of the Lord because it did not seem fair. Jonah soon sank into despondency. He actually wanted to end his life: "It is better for me to die than to live." (Jonah 4:8)

My nation, Great Britain, is obsessed with fairness. This is positive when it's about ensuring that the poorest people receive support. It can be a problem, though. If a co-worker being promoted sooner than me makes me feel wronged, it could delay, or even abort, my breakthrough. A friend getting their heart's desire before me should not provoke jealousy. Until I can rejoice in someone else's season of blessing, I am probably not ready for my own. The Lord has a unique plan for each one of us. That means different things will happen at different times and for different purposes.

# WHAT DID WE DO WRONG?

Early on in our ministry, my husband and I went through an upsetting trial. Accusations of betrayal were fired at us by an influential person. The accuser called each of our leaders one by one, telling them we were in rebellion. They then asked our over-seer to step us down immediately from ministry. Close friends distanced themselves and people who once admired us avoided eye contact. For a season, it felt like we had spiritual leprosy. When we walked into Christian conferences, we would find ourselves standing alone because no one wanted to be seen in our company. Not one of the allegations was true, but God told us not to try to defend ourselves. We had to keep our peace and leave our vindication to the Lord.

I was hurt by what was said, the way it was said and by who was saying it. I also felt betrayed by the people who believed the lies. It was all so unfair. I went to bed one night crushed and confused. I wanted to crawl into a hole and shut the world out. It felt as though someone had fired a dart straight into my heart. I was due to minister a day or two later so I knew I needed God's help, and quickly. The Holy Spirit brought this Scripture to mind: "Who can bear a broken spirit?" (Proverbs 18:14) I realized that something deep within was broken. I couldn't bear the pain.

Getting out of bed, I knelt down and called out to God. "I can't carry on while my heart is hurting so badly. This is not fair and it's not right." I cried in His presence and told the Lord what had pained me most. As I poured out my heart before Him, God tended my wounds. I felt the pain dislodge. It was then much easier to lay down the injustice of the situation. I went to bed tired, but relieved. I slept soundly and woke up the next morning at peace. The storm continued, yet I walked through it with dignity.

God has a way of turning trials into testimonies. Within two months, the Lord supernaturally revealed the truth and we were entirely vindicated. Genesis 35:3 says, "Let us arise and go up to Bethel and I will make an altar there to God who answered me in the day of my distress and has been with me in the way." We need to lay down injustice at the cross. Anger at the actions of others just makes things worse. We need to give it up in prayer. If anyone understands injustice, it is Jesus. Instead of feeling sorry for Himself, He pitied the people who wronged Him.

# A POISONOUS WEED IN SELF PITY'S BACK YARD

Self-pity is a breeding ground for one of the most common destiny-destroyers in the body of Christ: offense. Before going any further, let me explain the difference between hurt and offense. When we are hurt, we are wounded and we need healing. When we are offended, we are wounded or upset *and* we feel angry. If I am offended by something someone has done, I will want to shut them out. When I picture the person's face, I will feel some animosity. Offense is always followed up by some kind of corresponding action (see Mark 4).

Someone takes your place in the line. Your boss walks by without saying hello. Your friend leaves you stranded without a ride or you give your best and no one notices. Life is full of opportunities to be offended. Offense creates a sense of outrage or hurt. "How could she? It's not fair. That's not right." It usually starts small, with a thought. Job 4:12-13 unpacks how it happens: "Now a word was secretly brought to me and my ear received a whisper of it. In disquieting thoughts..." When someone whispers, it is because they would not want the world to hear what they are saying. Offense is like that. It usually starts with a whisper. We may feel slighted, cheated, ignored or undermined, but we would not want others to know how we feel at first.

The initial thought is not the offense - it is what we do with the thought. By rehearsing the incident, the whisper starts to disturb us. We recount what we wish we had said or what we think they should have done. Indignation builds. Offense normally comes from four directions. It is caused by what people say: cruel comments or rude remarks. And by what they do not say: no one thanks you for your labor of love or your husband fails to notice your hard work behind the scenes. Then it is prompted by what people do: someone takes your space in the parking lot when you are not looking or pushes you out of the way so that they can grab the last copy of the book you wanted. And by what they do not do: no one calls when you are sick, your friend does not visit when she said she would or your family forgets your birthday.

Let's stop here for a moment. None of us is perfect. We all make mistakes and unknowingly hurt one another. You will have done or said things that could have caused offense. Knowing that might help you to overlook the things that could cause you to become upset or angry. Loving others helps to keep us from offense. 1 Peter 4:8 (NLT) says, "Most important of all, continue to show deep love for each other, for love covers a multitude of sins." Having said that, another way to avoid offense is to stay on your healing journey. The more we are healed, the less we are wounded by the words or actions of others.

## THE PURPOSE

The parable of the sower in Mark 4:16-17 (Amplified) describes the purpose of offense: "The ones sown upon stony ground are those who... have no real root in themselves, and so they endure for a little while; then when trouble or persecution arises on account of the Word, they immediately are offended (become displeased, indignant, resentful) and they stumble and fall away."

Offense steals the word from our hearts. It makes us stumble and fall away. People have forsaken friends, left churches, quit jobs and resigned from positions - all because they were offended. You might be thinking, "Well why not? If you aren't happy, then move on!" That might sound convincing, but Romans 8:14 says that the sons of God are led by the Spirit of God, not by offense. Every time we are wounded, we need to get healed and forgive, *then* ask God for His will. If God tells us to move on, we can do it the right way: showing love and kindness to the people who hurt us.

Many years ago, we went through a painful season at church. A couple who had been in leadership for many years made a host of accusations against my husband and me. About a third of our congregation left. For a while, it seemed like everyone thought they could accuse us of anything. I was battered by the betrayal. A couple of months after it all happened, my family took off for a few days. One evening after the children had gone to bed, my husband asked me how I was doing. I remember my reply. "I feel like I've been marched onto the platform in our auditorium and stripped in front of everyone." I felt crushed and did not want to lead anymore. I loved Jesus, but I no longer liked the church.

## THREE WEEKS

My husband listened lovingly and then responded. "I am giving you three weeks to get healed. Our church needs a mother." As soon as we returned home, I got into the presence of God and poured out my pain in His presence. I told Him how much the words and actions of our people had hurt me. The Lord restored my heart and I forgave anyone who had wounded us. That's when the Lord showed me that it is impossible to really love the Lord and hate the church. Jesus is the head, but the church is *His* body. Any time I am angry with a Christian brother or sister, I am angry with one of God's children. 1 John 4:20 (NLT) says, 'If someone says, "I love God," but hates a fellow believer, that person is a liar; for if we don't love people we can see, how can we love God, whom we cannot see?" Once I was healed, it was much easier to deal with offenses. I am so glad that my husband insisted on me getting restored.

Offense is a test which every one of us has to pass again and again and again if we are going to fulfill our destiny. We might say that we are just angry or upset, but in truth, we are probably offended. Let me repeat again how to work out if you are hurt or if you are hurt *and* offended. When you consider the people who wronged you, how do you feel? If seeing their face in your mind's eye makes you cross, then you are probably not just hurt, but also offended. If our hurt is mixed with anger or injustice, then we are probably offended. Proverbs 14:10 says: "The heart knows its own bitterness..." Deep down, if we will admit it, we know when our hearts have grown hard towards particular people. That's a sure sign that we are offended.

## ALMOST IMPOSSIBLE

Proverbs 18:19 makes an extraordinary statement: "A brother offended is harder to win than a strong city..." I cannot imagine what it would take to overthrow a city! I am certain that I do not have the necessary skills or strength! Yet the Bible tells us that it is even harder to win over someone who is offended. Injustice often makes us hold tight to our offenses. If a brother is going to struggle to bring me back from the brink of offense, I am going to have to learn to spot it and expel it from my own life.

Offense breeds pride (that sense of superiority and judgment) and pride breeds offense. When we feel wronged, we all too easily harden our hearts. Others may try to offer correction, but we think they have no right. In other words, we batten down the hatches and push people away. You and I are the answer! We have to watch our own hearts like hawks. We have to learn to humble ourselves and accept the truth. We have to acknowledge that we will probably get offended from time to time. We need to be ready to spot faults in our own lives. It is a wonderful opportunity to kick pride out of our lives.

# THE WAY OUT

Part of the process of maturing in Christ is learning to love at the time when our flesh wants to react. Mark 4:17 says that we will be easily offended if we have *no real root*. In his letter to the church in Ephesus, Paul prayed that God's people would be *"... rooted and grounded in love..."* (Ephesians 3:17). Love enables us to overcome offense. Love is patient when people are unpleasant. It is kind to the callous and uncaring. If someone makes a mistake, love believes the best. It is not easily provoked, even by arrogant or rude behavior. Love never insists on its own rights, but it thinks about others first. Love covers. If my heart is full of this kind of love, then it will be very difficult for me to get offended. Love is the antidote to offense.

Hebrews 12:14 instructs us to: "Pursue peace with all people." That includes a bullying boss, a demanding mother-in-law, that difficult leader and so on. The only way to live at peace with people who have hurt us is to be healed and to forgive. When we are at peace, there is no anger or judgement. If you can work out what - or even who - presses your buttons, it will help you to be deliberate about guarding your heart from offense and instead choosing to love. Who makes you shake your head or causes your blood to boil? What kind of behaviors hurt you the most? Which types of people make you feel undermined? Ask God to give you extra grace for those situations.

# A DOSE OF TRUTH

You might be saying that you are not easily offended. Can I suggest that you ask the Holy Spirit for His opinion on that? According to the Bible, our hearts can (and do) lie to us. You see, it is easier to believe our view of ourselves than the truth because the truth is not always pretty. We do not know what is lurking inside. However, the Lord knows you and me better than we know ourselves. "The heart is deceitful above all things... Who can know it [perceive, understand, be acquainted with his own heart and mind]? I the Lord search the mind, I try the heart..." (Jeremiah 17:9-10 AMPC)

You may still feel that you are rarely offended. If so, praise God! However, there is one type of person that can offend even the unoffendable! Proverbs 23:17 in the Passion Translation says, "Don't allow the actions of evil men to cause you to burn with anger..." One group of people who can easily cause loving people to get offended are those who are easily offended themselves.

Guard yourself from becoming offended at offended people. Another scripture that makes this point is Proverbs 24:19: "Don't be angrily offended over evil-doers or be agitated by them" (TPT). Let's make sure that we show patience and kindness to those who are throwing one accusation after another our way. We need to be extra vigilant to protect our hearts when we are around people who push our buttons. Love and forgiveness are the opposite to offense so, as Colossians 3:14 instructs, "... put on love, which is the bond of perfection."

## WE NEVER KNOW

The day our two year old daughter died, we drove back from the hospital in a daze. We travelled very slowly in the fast lane. The driver behind us became very annoyed, beeping and flashing his lights at us. We moved out of his way. It taught me an important lesson. You never know what someone else is going through. Sometimes the way people are behaving is nothing to do with you or me and everything to do with their own difficult journey. I try to remember that.

If someone hurts your feelings, mistreats you or gets in your way, why not make a decision to be gracious and kind? It is amazing how much more enjoyable life is when we overlook the mistakes people make and give them the benefit of the doubt. Copy Jesus, who said, "I remember your sins no more." Let the offense go and put on love. If a neighbor does something that bothers you, overlook it for love's sake and be kind to them in return.

Proverbs 19:11 says, "The discretion of a man makes him slow to anger and his glory is to overlook a transgression." It is glorifying to God when we overlook being wronged. Overcoming offense forces us to be 'otherly'. It keeps our eyes off ourselves - something which is an antidote to self-pity. The more we conquer this enemy, the more we conquer self-pity. And the more we demolish self-pity, the easier it will be to overcome offense. Dealing with this foul destiny-destroyer might not be easy, but it is vital.

## THE BLAME GAME

Self-pity often seeks someone to blame. You might beat yourself up about your situation. You could hold someone else responsible. Maybe you've walked through a really tough time. Self-pity will try to tell you that no-one bothered to call. It will whisper that leaders were insensitive or that friends didn't care. It will look at the shortcomings of others during your time of trial. This only deepens the invisible trenches around us and makes our pain worse. A sense of injustice grows and relief feels further away. Something else happens too. When we blame others for part or even all of our misery, we relinquish control of our own happiness. We give others the keys to our wellbeing.

Let's look at what goes on inside when we decide to blame someone. We are usually irritated or angry because we feel wronged. Our eyes are on the errors of others. All too often, blame is rooted in judgement. When we judge, it injures us more than those we hold responsible. Matthew 7:1-2 (AMPC) says, "Do not judge and criticize and condemn others... For just as you judge and criticize and condemn others, you will be judged and criticized and condemned, and in accordance with the measure you [use to] deal out to others, it will be dealt out again to you."

When I judge someone for the way they treat me, I open the door for others to criticize me when I get it wrong. I regularly make mistakes. When this happens, I want friends and family to overlook my errors. I want them to be merciful. Mercy is simply being kind to people who don't deserve it. If I want others to be gracious with me, I need to be kind to the people who let me down. I need to overlook their wrongs. Blame stirs anger and frustration, whereas mercy releases love and peace. Although it may be hard on our flesh for a moment, mercy feels great afterwards!

# DEFLECTION

Since the start of time, man has used blame to deflect truth and God's conviction. Adam's first instinct was to blame God and his wife when he was confronted about his sin. Let's look at Genesis 3:12: 'Then the man said, "The woman whom You gave to be with me, she gave me of the tree, and I ate."' Adam blamed God for giving him Eve. Then he blamed Eve for giving him the forbidden fruit. You can almost hear the sentiment behind his words. "It's not fair. I didn't ask for a woman. I didn't choose her. It's not my fault. I'm just a victim stuck in the middle." I wonder whether history may have told a different story if Adam had instead immediately accepted responsibility for his mistakes? Blame got him nowhere.

You may not have done anything for which you need to take responsibility. You could be the victim of horrific circumstances.

Irrespective of our innocence, we have a choice about whether we blame others. 1 Peter 4:8 (AMPC) says, "... Love covers a multitude of sins [forgives and disregards the offenses of others]." Blame rehearses the wrongs of others. Love overlooks them. The latter might sound extremely difficult, but it definitely helps us on the road to recovery. We set ourselves free from the very people we were holding responsible. Let's pray:

**Heavenly Father,**

Sometimes life feels so unfair. I have been through a great deal as a result of the wrongs of others. (*Now tell the Lord about any pain you feel. Explain what happened and how it affected you. Be as specific as possible.*) I ask You to take my pain away and heal my heart. I realize that I also have allowed my suffering to make me feel sorry for myself. I felt wronged and angry. (*Now share with the Lord about any self-pity or offense that has been hiding in your heart. Ask Him to forgive you for holding anger.*)

Lord, where I have blamed people in the past, I choose today to take my eyes off their wrongs and instead to look to You for my freedom and healing. I ask You to expose any self-absorption in my thinking. I give You any sense of entitlement that I have held. I lay down every offense, every judgement, every anger, and all blame. You alone are qualified to judge! I choose to overlook the wrongs of others and even the wrongs of life itself. Fill me afresh with Your wonderful love. Thank You that You have brought me this far. Thank You that You have great plans for my life. I love You with all of my heart.

In Jesus' name, I pray,

Amen.

# Part Two

# THE WEAPONS

Self-pity sneaks up on us. It whispers lies in our ears that sound like the truth. It convinces us that it is the only one who really cares so we open up to its schemes. Our pretend friend has many weapons to lure us into its world. In section two, we will expose three of self-pity's most common tactics.

# Chapter 5

# INNER WHISPERS

Negative thoughts give self-pity its power. They drain your joy and drag you down. The enemy works overtime to sow pessimism in your mind. He whispers lies in your ears, hoping that you will believe his spin. Maybe you recognize some of these sentiments: "I can't handle this anymore," "Life is too hard," "Everything is stacked against me," "This is too painful," "Nobody understands what I'm going through," "My life sucks," or "Nothing ever works out for me." Let's remind ourselves of what Job 5:7 says: "...man is born to trouble..." This means that you and I will face pain again - regardless of whether we are in it right now.

When we are in a stressful season, the temptation to give in intensifies. Even when all is well, this foul foe knocks on our door. All it takes is a bad cold or an unexpected bill and negativity tries to creep in. As we embark on this journey together, why not decide now that you will start to filter your thoughts? If you are in the middle of a fiery trial, learning these lessons will help you come out the other side as quickly as possible.

## IT'S NOT THAT DEEP (OR IS IT?)

The enemy is always seeking to pull us down by influencing our thinking. Proverbs 23:7 explains that what we meditate on shapes our lives: "As a man thinks in his heart, so is he." In other words, we are a product of our inner thoughts. Heart thoughts aren't just the ideas buzzing around your mind. They include your inner convictions and your beliefs about yourself and the world. These deep assumptions profoundly affect your life. In my book My Whole Heart, I explain how you can transform your heart thoughts so that they become building blocks instead of barricades.

Head thoughts aren't always linked to what we believe, but they still affect our moods and attitudes. Just allowing one simple thought into your mind - "It's not fair," for example - will almost always dampen your spirits. Furthermore, when something occupies your thoughts for long enough, it can start to shape your convictions. I hear the phrase, "It's not that deep!" batted about all the time. It is easy to minimize the impact of fleeting thoughts. However, every single one of these influences your life to some extent. If you learn to master your thoughts, you will be amazed at the changes in every area of your life. Romans 12:2b (NLT) says, "... let God transform you into a new person by changing the way you think..." It requires commitment, but it is well worth the effort.

Keep your heart open as you read and allow the Lord to expose any unhelpful habits. Once you are aware of negative ideas, it will be easier to stop them in their tracks. Awareness is the first step. We will cover four different types of thinking. Search for yourself in the paragraphs that follow so that you can conquer thought patterns that may hamper your life.

# 1. YOUR DAILY COMMENTARY

Can you relate to any of the following scenarios? You spill your coffee and wonder, "Why am I so stupid?" Someone cuts you off in traffic and you think, "It's going to be one of those days!" Your boss doesn't like your work and you tell yourself, "I'm never going to make it." A friend cancels a meeting and you say, "No one really likes me." We will get back to these statements in a moment.

Let me ask you if you have ever watched a sports game on television alongside an avid fan. They probably talk to the TV throughout the match. Maybe they yell when tension rises! Or you could be that fan and you know exactly what I'm talking about! You are probably not a serious expert and yet that never stopped anyone having an opinion. Just like a sports commentator scrutinizes every move of every player, most of us comment on even the most inconsequential events in our lives. There is an inner commentary that most of us listen to. We don't even question what we are hearing.

Let us look at the truth of the inner reactions I mentioned in the previous paragraph. Spilling your coffee just means that you spilt your coffee. It does not have anything to do with your intelligence - even if you do it regularly. Maybe the lid needs to be tightened tomorrow? Someone cutting you off in traffic is not an indicator of something. It has no power to affect your day - unless you give it permission. Difficult feedback does not mean you won't make it. In fact, learning from mistakes is one of the best ways to grow. Being let down does not say anything about your popularity. It suggests that your friend made a mistake.

## SNOWBALLING

The problem can be made worse by the snowball effect. One negative whisper often triggers an avalanche of condemnation. Wondering, "Why am I so stupid?" leads to: "I never get anything right. I can't even drink my coffee without messing up..." Maybe you go further: "What's the point in even trying?" If we don't stop the negativity, it drags us down. The commentary influences our attitudes and sets our mood. You may have been okay when you woke up, but before you know it, you're disillusioned. Proverbs 23:7 says, "As a man thinks in his heart, so is he..." Our thoughts (even about everyday issues) shape our outlook on life. Late trains, bad traffic and busy streets can only affect our attitudes if we listen to the negative commentaries.

Our moods don't just affect us. They have an impact on others as well. If you listen to the negative commentary, you may walk into work feeling down or annoyed. When a manager is considering who to promote, they will probably be more likely to pick someone who is positive. Romans 12:2 says, "Don't copy the behavior and customs of this world, but let God transform you into a new person by changing the way you think..." Challenging negativity and then choosing to think the right thoughts will change your life.

You can choose what you listen to and you can silence negative commentaries. The first step is realizing that you have an inner commentator! Once you realize that voice can try to negatively interpret even unimportant events, you can start the process of shutting it down. Once you are aware of that commentary, I encourage you to speak back! If you hear an inner voice saying, "You get everything wrong," you can reply: "Actually I get lots of things right!" If you hear the suggestion, "Oh no, it looks like today is going to be a bad day," you can retort: "No. Today is the day that the Lord has made. I will rejoice because today will be a great day!" We can get through even difficult seasons in victory if we filter our thoughts.

# 2. COMPLAINING

I have heard preachers say that the language of hope is dreams. In other words, I constantly talk about my dreams coming to pass when I am full of Bible hope. I believe that the language of self-pity is complaint. If I am feeling sorry for myself, I will moan and complain much of the time. Just as gratitude is an attitude that starts in our hearts, so complaining begins when no one else can hear what we are saying to ourselves. But here's the thing: God is always listening.

One wet day in November, I returned from my morning run. My husband asked me how it went. I said, "It was very muddy. There was a lot of rain last night." He continued: "But did you enjoy yourself?" A little confused, I replied, "It was wet!" He paused and then he challenged me: "You have a default towards negativity! Why can't you just tell me you had a wonderful run?"

I didn't like what he was saying, but I realized that he was right. Have you ever picked up a shopping cart at the grocery store only to find that your trolley has a wonky wheel? You have to work extra hard to keep it from veering to the left or the right. Just like that cart, I realized that I had a tendency to be negative. I veered too easily into gloom. I didn't want people to think I was enjoying life too much in case they expected more from me. I saw life being tough as a ticket to special concessions. I worked hard to change my default setting and soon found life more enjoyable.

In Britain, we have an awful habit. When people ask us how we are, a classic response is: "Not too bad." It's a means of saying that we are okay, but it is harmful because it is negative. Listen to the way you think about your life. Do you often feel cheated or let down? Do you complain in your heart when people are late or you have to wait? Do you get irritated with other drivers? Are you unhappy when you don't get your way? When we moan our way through the day, it quenches our joy. Our pretend friend feels very much at home when we are complaining.

# IF IT'S TOO MUCH

I have heard people say, "New levels bring new devils." They are making the point that the higher we rise, the greater the potential for pressure. A chief executive carries a heavier weight of responsibility than an executive trainee. If my reaction to every trial at a junior level is bewilderment then perhaps I am not ready for promotion? If I moan every time things get tough now then I may need to spend longer at this stage learning how to handle things.

If you realize your reactions need to change, I want to encourage you to filter your thoughts and watch your words. We can change our reactions. Proverbs 15:15 in The Passion Translation is very revealing: "Everything seems to go wrong when you feel weak and depressed. But when you choose to be cheerful, every day will bring you more and more joy and fullness." We can choose our attitude and our mood and that will probably help us prepare for promotion.

# 3. SAD THOUGHTS

Some time ago, I really hurt my husband. For a while, he completely shut down towards me. This in turn bruised me. Every time I saw a happy couple, I felt a stabbing pain. Their smiles reminded me of my own shortcomings. I remember scrolling down my social media newsfeed and seeing a man's passionate tribute to his wife on their anniversary. It felt like an arrow to my heart. Their matrimonial success told me that I was a failure.

Then God spoke to me. He said sorrow would not change anything, but faith would. In the same way that I had for years taken captive thoughts of pride or offense, I had to learn to deal with sadness. Anytime it rose up on the inside of me, I forcefully took hold of my thoughts and reminded myself of the faithfulness of God. Instead of allowing my feelings to spiral, I chose to focus on God's promises. Each time I did, faith grew in my heart.

Sad thoughts focus on the hopelessness of a situation. They rehearse hurts and pull you down further. They seem harmless, but they can be crippling because they magnify pain. Maybe it hurts when you see people enjoying what you have lost. If your marriage is in crisis, happy couples may make you recoil. If you lost your job, testimonies about promotions can be unbearable.

Remember that faith grows in our hearts. Romans 10:10 says, "... with your heart you believe..." (Berean Study Bible) so we need to watch what we nurture inside. If I allow sadness to settle in my soul then it will be hard for faith to arise. It is better for us to pour out our pain in prayer. Then lift our eyes from our circumstances and focus on the promises of God.

# OVERWHELM

When we are living with emotional pain, the sadness can be overwhelming. You may even have a knot in your stomach as you read this. Perhaps you have been betrayed by someone you love. Maybe you have experienced a broken marriage. You could be going through some other agony. If that's you, you need to be healed. We have seen countless men and women experience life-changing restoration at our Healed for Life conferences. You too can be made whole, even after terrible tragedy. Many of us treat our cars better than we do our hearts. Please prioritize your inner well-being for the sake of your future. Getting healed will help you come out the other side strong. I will repeat this many times throughout this book, and there is a chapter dedicated to your healing in part three.

Getting healed is not all we need to do, though. When we are troubled, various negative voices compete for our attention.

There are thoughts of despair that tell us we will never find our way out. They make us focus on the tragedy of our situation. There are negative mindsets that program us to expect disappointment or difficulty. Our pretend friend tells us that all of the above are appropriate and inevitable. Please know that this is not true. Colossians 1:21 explains that our thoughts can separate us from what God has for us: "And you, who once were alienated and enemies in your mind..." Thoughts can be our worst enemies in difficult times. Becoming aware of wrong ideas is the first step to silencing them. Why not write down any common thought patterns that you identify as you read? We will then deal with them at the end of this chapter.

# 4. HAPPY FAMILIES

You may try to avoid classic pictures of happiness on social media or in films. If you are in a bad relationship, then images of happy families may hurt. If you lost your job or your ministry is failing then sights of others succeeding may sting. You may want to turn away to avoid the pain. However, I want you to know that this is unhelpful in the long run.

The cause of such discomfort is often fear. We are afraid of feeling the pain again. The problem is that fear of anything gives the object of our fear power in our lives. For example, if I am afraid of spiders, I give spiders the power to intimidate me and even control my behavior. Fear almost always makes matters worse. You don't have to be afraid of anything from your past. No memory or sight should have the power to make you flinch.

When I was engaged, everywhere I looked I saw women wearing rings! When I was pregnant, I saw expectant moms all around me. What is my point? We tend to see the world through the filter of our own lives. If your marriage is rocky, you will probably keep seeing loving couples. If you lost a child, you will most likely see little ones everywhere you look. As a result, you will have lots of opportunities to feel threatened by images. Fear wants you to turn away in greater pain. But what if the very images that created angst could instead bring you to healing or create hope? Let's deal with healing first.

# TURNING IT AROUND

If you have been hurt or bereaved, I encourage you to let images of others enjoying what you lost lead you to times of healing. When you see something that might make you recoil in fear, please don't turn away. Instead, bring that picture before God in prayer. As Lamentations 2:19 says, "Pour out your heart like water before the face of the Lord." Tell Him how you feel and describe what is going on inside. In Isaiah 9:6, we are told that Jesus is our Wonderful Counsellor. The purpose of counselling is to offload our burdens and share our secret pain. When we do that with our Savior, we will experience His wonderful healing. That's what I call supernatural counselling! Don't let fear make you turn away. Instead, look at images that hurt and bring God into your experience. Tell Him about the pain and keep asking Him to heal you. In part three of this book, we will spend plenty of time helping you to heal.

# FRESH HOPE

Now let's look at how images that once made you shudder can instead breathe fresh hope into your heart. Psalms 123:1-2 says, "Unto You I lift up my eyes, O You who dwell in the heavens. Behold, as the eyes of servants look to the hand of their masters, as the eyes of a maid to the hand of her mistress, so our eyes look to the Lord our God, until He has mercy on us." When someone else's success makes you feel like a failure, please be quick to lift up your eyes to the Lord. Instead of turning away in sadness from someone else's happiness, why not allow those images to stir your faith? If you are lonely, when you see people loving and laughing, choose to believe for your breakthrough. Don't let intimidating images make your situation worse. Invite God in and turn every picture you see into a point of contact for your faith.

A while back, I was flicking through social media when I saw a photo of a friend. She was pictured doing exactly what I had been believing God for years to achieve. Although I was genuinely delighted for her, I was deeply discouraged and felt like a fool. A barrage of thoughts bombarded my mind: "I bet she never cut out pictures and put them in her dream book!" (Yes, that's right, I did and I have the book to prove it!). Her success made me doubt myself. I wondered why I was always falling short of my hopes and expectations. I got into the presence of God and started to pray, telling the Lord how I felt.

## THE SPIN DOCTOR

Almost immediately, I felt a check in my spirit. I was listening to the lies of our pretend friend, the spin doctor. The devil whispers untruths in our ears. He spins the stories of our circumstances to paint a discouraging picture. The Holy Spirit reminded me that God shows no partiality (Acts 10:34). What He does for one, He will gladly do for another. The very picture which God showed me to encourage me the devil used to drag me down. As I sat in His presence, I apologized. I had allowed myself to be deceived by the devil and pulled into a state of discouragement and self-pity. So I started to encourage myself in the Lord instead.

## DO IT AGAIN!

I declared boldly, "Father, you are always faithful! Thank you for my sister's great success. I rejoice with her. I see it as a sign that my breakthrough is around the corner." In the Hebrew, the root meaning of the word testify is actually "do it again"! We are instructed to tell other people when God is good to us because it creates an atmosphere for more miracles. Every time a brother or sister shares their glory story, after we have celebrated their miracle, we can respond to God: "Do it again, Lord!"

I do not know how long you have been waiting for God to fulfill His promises. Maybe things have happened around you that have discouraged you. Perhaps satan has been warping the story and telling you it will never take place. You don't have to listen to negative thoughts. Remember, although Abraham waited for 25 years, he became the father of faith and had his son. Despite suffering terribly for 13 years, Joseph's dreams came to pass and he was promoted to the position of prime minister. Do not let the enemy tell tales about your circumstances. While you are praying and believing, God is at work behind the scenes to prepare the stage for your success.

## WE GET TO CHOOSE

Philippians 4:8 in the Amplified says, "... whatever is true, whatever is worthy of reverence and is honorable and seemly, whatever is just, whatever is pure, whatever is lovely and lovable, whatever is kind and winsome and gracious, if there is any virtue and excellence, if there is anything worthy of praise, think on and weigh and take account of these things [fix your minds on them]." This verse tells us to filter the ideas that bombard our minds. It urges us to select helpful thought patterns. Remember, this is not about pushing pain down. We need to give every hurt to God in prayer. This is about deciding that we won't allow sadness to dominate our souls.

Just as you and I can choose not to think critical or unkind thoughts, we can also decide not to dwell on our problems. I like the last phrase in the verse which instructs us to think on, weigh and take account of the good around us. When we take account of something, we look at it in detail. This scripture is telling us to be intentional about seeing blessings in our lives.

Sad thoughts aren't just a problem during trials or tragedies. They can try to pull us down even when life is good. I picked up my iPad to write while I was traveling recently. As I looked out of the airplane window, my children felt painfully far away. I ached to be back home hearing about their days at school. Then I started to long to be with my husband. Before I knew it, my heart was sinking. I had succumbed to one of self-pity's trusted weapons: sad thoughts. I quickly pulled myself together, reminded myself of the privilege of ministry and spent some time thanking God for His goodness to me and my family. Melancholia evaporated almost as quickly as it had descended. You have the same power to dispel thoughts by filtering your thinking. It's a game-changer.

## 5. THE SYMPATHY TICKET

When I first got married, I used to open up to any sickness that knocked at my door. My throat might start to scratch and I would think to myself, "Oh dear, I'm coming down with a cold." I would feel a little sorry for myself, then tell my husband Paul that I wasn't very well. I wanted him to be extra attentive. I saw sickness as a sympathy ticket and I wanted to cash in. I really believed I deserved to be pitied and pampered. However, my husband had a different perspective. He hated any kind of illness. He saw disease as an enemy that needed to be crushed beneath our feet. Whenever a cold tried to creep up on my husband, he would blast it away with the Word of God. Even if he had to fight for several days, Paul never gave up until he was in top form again.

When I felt ill, I wanted Paul's sympathy but he refused to indulge sickness. There were times when I thought he was being mean. Proverbs 27:6 says, "Faithful are the wounds of a friend, but the kisses of an enemy are deceitful." He was not irritated by me being unwell. He was annoyed that I was taking it lying down. He wanted me to fight by faith, but that is difficult when you are feeling sorry for yourself. After a couple of years of marriage, I began to understand. He told me how he responded to symptoms. "From the first moment I feel a tickle in my throat or nose, I start declaring the Word of God over my body. Bible verses go round my mind non-stop until the sickness backs off." I learned to do likewise. Paul's refusal to pity me was maturing me into a woman of faith.

# 6. 'NO-GO' MEMORIES

Certain memories can be shut away in 'no-go' rooms hidden in the vast expanses of our hearts. We dare not open the doors of those rooms because the contents are too painful. When something opens the door, we try to turn our faces away so that we don't have to witness the sight, feel the pain or experience the shame again. We think that by avoiding those recollections, we are helping ourselves to recover or preventing self-pity.

The problem is that if you avoid certain memories, the enemy can use them to trip you up whenever he chooses. He can create a flashback whenever he likes. As a result, we end up just as afraid of those memories as we were of the pain that caused them in the first place. And as we know, fear is an enemy of God. The Bible explains that God desires to search even painful places because His will is always to bring healing and freedom. Proverbs 20:27 says, "The spirit of a man is the lamp of the Lord, searching all the inner depths of his heart." The Hebrew word for inner depths is *heder* and it means apartment, inner chamber or cavern. Your heart is like a vast mansion with many rooms. The Lord wants to search out pain: He reveals in order to heal.

# SPINNING

There are certain memories that used to hold me bound. I would try to turn away to stop myself from experiencing the pain of the past again. When I woke up on the days immediately after our daughter died, I would sometimes forget the loss for a few moments. The thing that usually reminded me of her death was the empty space in the corner of our bedroom where her baby listening monitor used to sit. Somehow that sight had the power to send me into a spin.

I would first remember my little girl lying unwell on my tummy in the middle of the night. I would remember my fear and think about her sweet body snuggling close to mine. Then I would soon find myself back in that horrible place of panic and despair, not knowing what to do. Soon, I would see her asleep in the morning as I went to work. I would watch myself leave the house. Next, I would be on the train to work and I would hear that mobile phone call with my husband and the angst in our voices.

Finally, I would receive that message. Naomi had been rushed to hospital in an ambulance and I must leave work immediately. I would see the corner of the meeting room where I was standing as I listened to that fateful voicemail message. I got to the hospital as quickly as possible, but the rest is history. Once or twice the memories sucked me into such deep dread that I suffered a panic attack. There have been other memory cycles that have gripped me at different times of my life as well.

# THE WAY OUT

I met a doctor who ran a training session for leaders about ministering to people who suffer from panic attacks. I remember silently weeping my way through the down-to-earth workshop. I learned an important lesson that day. While we run away from painful memories, we stay bound by the fear of those events. If you ever get flashbacks, I encourage you to face the inner pictures that have tormented you. If you regularly turn away from certain memories, please rethink your reactions.

Fear's power is fear. The Bible puts it this way: "...fear involves torment..." (1 John 4:18). Let me explain. When we are afraid of particular memories, it is fear itself that makes those thoughts frightening. When we eliminate fear, we can look at the pictures that once tormented us and get healed of the hurt instead. The pain goes away and those memories lose their sting. When you face past agony, you remove fear and can focus on restoration.

Next time someone or something opens the door to that room in your heart, don't run away. Instead, invite the Holy Spirit to come in and ask Jesus to heal you of the pain of that memory. Look at the pictures of your past. Examine the memories that try to over-whelm you. Tell the Lord how much they hurt and why.

After that workshop by the Christian doctor, I brought every painful memory to Jesus and I asked Him to heal my heart, piece by piece. I told Him I would never again be afraid of facing difficult experiences. From that moment onwards, I brought every picture to Him when it came to mind. I was never again sucked into a downward spiral of flashbacks and I never again had a panic attack. I was not yet whole, but I was getting healed.

## WHERE DID THAT COME FROM?

Remember that not all your thoughts were originally yours! The enemy seeks to plant ideas in your mind. In truth, it doesn't matter how the thoughts reached your mind. It matters that you get the wrong ones out. "Casting down arguments and every high thing that exalts itself against the knowledge of God, bringing every thought into captivity to the obedience of Christ." (2 Corinthians 10:5). When we cast something, we hurl or throw it. There is force behind our actions. We need to capture and kick out negative thoughts.

The verse tells us to bring wrong ideas into captivity. I don't know about you, but I associate captivity with criminality. It makes me think I should look at negativity the same way I would look at a burglar trying to break into my home. Just as a robber wants to take your things, pessimism tries to steal your hope and your faith. Why not stamp out melancholy? Ask yourself the question, "Where did that come from?" and then kick all negativity out as though you were throwing thieves out of your house.

## WHEN THOUGHTS TURN TO TALK

Some things are inevitable. Matthew 12:34b (NLT) says, "... whatever is in your heart determines what you say." When you allow your thoughts to linger, eventually they will come out of your mouth. That is even more serious. Our thoughts affect our lives and our words seal the deal. The Bible says that our words shape our lives. We are made in the image of God who said, "'Let there be light"; and there was light' (Genesis 1:3). Our words have the power to bring death and life (see Proverbs 18:21).

All speech is powerful, but we believe what we tell ourselves more than we believe what others say. What you whisper under your breath about your own ability matters more than you may realize. Your assessment of your efforts counts. When life is tough, we need to be even more watchful over what we pronounce about our lives. Proverbs 15:4b in TPT says, "...negative words do nothing but crush..." I encourage you to become aware of what you say to yourself. It may be out loud. It could be under your breath. Whatever you say, make sure it helps you. It is always easier to go with negativity, but when you stop those statements and replace them with the truth, you will reap the benefits.

## POINTLESS WORDS

A while ago, I sank into a hole that I dug for myself in the run up to one of my conferences. The contract was signed, but bookings were few. I knew that lives were being transformed through the ministry so I could not understand why people were staying away in their thousands! After a week of introspection, I began to talk to a few people. My conversations started something like this: "I don't know what else I can do. I've given my all." Or: "I've got my name on that contract. It is my head on the line!"

Everything coming out of my mouth was designed to extract sympathy. I did not realize what I was doing at the time, but I wanted others to understand how difficult it was being *me*. I wanted their pity. It is not just what we say, but how we say it. There is often a whimpering tone in our voice when we want attention because of our struggles. In contrast, David reacted to difficulty by encouraging himself. Instead of seeking support from others, he built himself back up. 1 Samuel 30:6 says, "Now David was greatly distressed, for the people spoke of stoning him... But David strengthened himself in the Lord his God." In the midst of the battle, the psalmist reminded himself of the faithfulness of God. He talked to himself in such a way that he ended up encouraged.

## IDLE WORDS

When I first got married, my husband worked hard to get me to pay attention to every throwaway comment. I would regularly make statements like: "I'm sick of work," or: "I'm afraid I can't make it." He asked me to get sickness and fear out of my conversation. To me, these were harmless references, and he was overreacting. However, out of respect for my husband, I stopped using these phrases. I really didn't believe they mattered that much. That was until I looked more closely at my Bible.

I mentioned Naomi's tragedy (which is told in the book of Ruth in the Old Testament) in chapter three. Let's go back to that story again. Naomi was married to a man called Elimelech and they had two sons. They moved as a family to Moab to avoid a famine in Judah. However, while they were in Moab, Naomi lost her husband and both of her boys. It is likely that Elimelech died as an old man, but why would Naomi's sons die young? Ruth 1:2 tells us that the name of one was Mahlon and the other was Chilion. Mahlon means sick and Chilion means pining. Day after day, year after year, Naomi (and lots of others) would have called these boys by their names. Sickness and pining were declared constantly over these young men. I am convinced that they were killed by words, even if disease or disaster eventually pulled the trigger. I'm sure that no one meant to do any harm. They were just saying their names.

## CERTAIN WORDS

Several years ago, I eliminated two words from my vocabulary. I banned myself from saying that I was *busy* or that I was *tired*. I noticed that these words seemed to make matters worse. Just saying, "I am tired," fuels self-pity and sounds wearying! Similarly, telling ourselves (or others) that we are busy sounds burdensome. Jesus had just three years of ministry to set the stage for the whole world to be saved - but He never gave the impression that He was overworked! His mindset was different. He believed that there were enough hours in the day and that He had the time He needed to get the job done. Jesus never suggested that He was even in a rush! I believe we can learn from His example.

If I have been on the go for a long time, telling myself and others that I am tired does not renew my strength. In fact, it makes things worse. It becomes a self-fulfilling prophecy. Proverbs 18:21 says, "Death and life are in the power of the tongue." Our words can drag us down or we can use them to breathe life into our lives. Joel 3:10b provides us with a powerful principle. It reads: "Let the weak say, 'I am strong.'" By faith, we can declare what we are believing to receive from God. Instead of moaning that I'm overwhelmed, I can look to the Lord and proclaim, "Thank You, Lord, that I can do all things through Christ who strengthens me." Self-pity prefers it if we rehearse our problems and talk about how tired we are. This only makes things worse.

I am not suggesting that we deny the truth. However, to say, "I need to get some rest," is far more positive than agreeing with exhaustion. Your words are seeds and they influence your attitude. Some thoughts cultivate an atmosphere in which self-pity thrives. What pulls me down might be different to what affects you, but there are probably some common threads: "I'm tired", "I've got too much to do", "Not again", "It's not fair", "This is too much", or, "It's one thing after another." I encourage you to listen to your language and pay attention to the impact it has on your disposition. We can help set our attitude by the thoughts that we think and the words that we say.

## ENABLERS

You may have heard of the idea of an enabler in a drug addict's life. That is someone who (probably unwittingly) facilitates an addict's habit. Maybe it makes the enabler feel needed or valuable. I think that there are enablers in the area of self-pity. Their reactions to our suffering will include statements like, "Oh no, poor you. That's awful." An enabler may reinforce our feelings and join our pity party. They may be motivated by compassion, but their reaction to our situation can make it even harder for us to break free. Even prayer requests can sometimes make matters worse. Instead of injecting faith into our hearts, a friend may focus on the sorry state of our situation and mix that together with a little too much sympathy.

Sometimes we are the enablers. Our concern about the situations others face may make them more likely to wallow than fight. If we care about a person, we need to assess what's best for them. If a brother or sister has a tendency towards self-pity, then you would do well to focus on building their faith when they are in difficulty. Resist the temptation to look worried and instead remind them of the power of God to turn their lives around.

Filtering your thoughts is one of the most transformative habits you can develop. Let's look again at Romans 12:2b (Passion Translation): "... be inwardly transformed by the Holy Spirit through a total reformation of how you think. This will empower you to discern God's will as you live a beautiful life, satisfying and perfect in his eyes." Although you will need to make a concerted effort, it is possible for anyone to change their thought life. Take captive wrong thoughts the moment you notice them. Then replace negativity and sadness with faith-filled truths. Let's pray:

**Heavenly Father,**

I realize that I have allowed a whole host of negative thoughts to influence my life. Firstly, I ask for Your forgiveness for dwelling on doubt and unbelief. Lord, I pray that You will cleanse my mind of all unnecessary sadness and gloom. I pray that You will help me to hear wrong thoughts so that I can shut them down. Make me aware of my inner commentary and give me the courage to answer back with Your Word. Holy Spirit, I ask for Your help to change the way I think. I don't want to entertain thoughts that will bind me in self-pity. I want to think faith-filled thoughts that reflect what the Bible says. Help me to trash negativity and instead to meditate on things that are true, honorable, right, pure, lovely and admirable. Enable me to dwell on things that are excellent and worthy of praise.

In Jesus' name, I pray,

Amen.

# Chapter 6

# LIES

Your pretend friend knows you. The whispers you hear are normally a subtle combination of truth and lies. That is what makes its arguments a little too easy to believe. It may be true that you have been terribly hurt, but it is not true that the ache will always remain. It may be fair to say that you're in a bad place. That does not mean you're in a bleak place. The former recognizes the difficulty of your situation. The latter wrongly suggests that there is no hope.

Ezekiel 13:22 says, "...with lies you have made the heart of the righteous sad, whom I have not made sad..." I encourage you to stop for a moment right now and assess what you are allowing into your mind. Are your thoughts a reflection of the truth or are they a negative distortion of reality? Are they helping you or are they making things worse? I am not suggesting you should bottle up your feelings. That is unhealthy. But you choose what you dwell on. There is no doubt that the truth will always help you, whereas pessimism will pull you down.

In the midst of challenging seasons, subtle lies can creep into our thinking. They may sound something like this: "I can't take this pain anymore", "I have messed everything up", "This is too much for me", or, "There is no way out". The enemy uses lies like these to amplify our agony and drag us into self-pity. All sorts of unhelpful sentiments can rise up inside us. Such reactions may be understandable. However, that does not make them accurate. One thing is for sure. They will only take you in one direction - and that is down.

Remember, we can choose what we think. We can decide whether or not we listen to the devil. Our enemy is a master liar: it's who he is and lying is what he does. Nothing he says to you is ever true because "...there is no truth in him..." (John 8:44b). He also has a host of demons that work for him and whisper untruths into believers' ears. We need to be vigilant about what we allow into our minds.

Although satan tells lots of lies, there are certain trusted distortions that he regularly throws at Christians - especially when life is tough. Ecclesiastes 1:9 says, "That which has been is what will be, that which is done is what will be done, and there is nothing new under the sun." In short, the devil does not have any new tricks! He has a few 'go-to' lies that he throws at us when we are struggling. Our pretend friend loves to whisper these in our ears. Let's look at four of them one by one.

## LIE NUMBER ONE: "I CAN'T COPE"

You may be tempted to think that you can't cope in distressing seasons. There may be challenges coming at you from every direction. Maybe you are feeling overwhelmed. But that does not mean that you cannot cope. In fact, this common sentiment contradicts the Word of God and God cannot lie (see Hebrews 6:18). Philippians 4:13 in the Amplified is crystal clear: "I have strength for all things in Christ Who empowers me [I am ready for anything and equal to anything through Him Who infuses inner strength into me; I am self-sufficient in Christ's sufficiency]."

This verse is powerful and it proves that you and I *can* cope. With the help of the Holy Spirit, you and I *can* handle even terrible difficulties. The verse begins with an extraordinary statement: "I have strength for all things in Christ..." When the Bible says all, it means all. It is easy to read scripture through a filter and somehow think that such a statement only applies in certain circumstances. This is not the case.

You and I can get through any and every situation as long as we rely on the Lord. You can cope, but you need to choose which ideas you allow to dominate your mind. You are the referee who decides whether ideas racing through your mind are good or bad. If you rehearse sentiments like, 'I can't cope,' your thoughts will wear you down and they may erode what strength you have. In tough times more than ever, we need to carefully filter our thoughts. We need to expose and reject any lies that we are listening to.

After my American spiritual mom passed away, I remember crying out as anguish filled my heart, "I can't cope with this!" It wasn't long before I realized that I was repeating a lie from the enemy. I corrected myself and thanked God that I had enough strength for every season. 2 Timothy 4:5 says, "But you be watchful in all things, endure afflictions..." With God's help we have the capacity to endure any difficulty and to come out the other side strong.

## THIS IS TOO MUCH

In the same vein, we can easily believe the lie that our load is too heavy. I have often believed that I was facing more than my fair share of suffering. How could I be kicked again when I was already down? There have been times when it felt like life itself was laughing at me! The problem is that when we believe ideas like these, we make matters even worse. Let me show you how...

Shut your eyes and say, "This is too much!" to yourself right now. Pay attention to how this statement makes you feel. It probably projected negativity. Perhaps you felt heaviness descend. It may have created a sense of despondency. Remember that the words we say to ourselves have the power to either build us up or tear us down (Proverbs 18:21). In the parable of the sower, Jesus taught that the Word of God is like seed that is sown in the ground. We are made in His image so our words are also seeds that either produce fruit or weeds.

1 Corinthians 10:13 in the Passion Translation says, "We all experience times of testing, which is normal for every human being. But God will be faithful to you. He will screen and filter the severity, nature, and timing of every test or trial you face so that you can bear it. And each test is an opportunity to trust him more, for along with every trial God has provided for you a way of escape that will bring you out of it victoriously."

The first part of this verse says that we all go through tough times. Far from being unfair or unusual, difficulty is normal! In addition, God will not allow us to be tested beyond what we can handle. It says that He will ensure that, "... you *can* bear it." The second part adds that the Lord always makes a way out of the pain and strain. You don't have to listen to the lie that your load is too heavy - it will only make things worse.

Ecclesiastes 1:9 reminds us that there is nothing new under the sun. Countless others have suffered just like you and me. As they have come out strong, so can we. It was not too much for them and it is not too much for you or me. I can tell you with all certainty that we grow more in the valleys than we do on the mountain tops. You can handle this season if you believe the Word, remain prayerful and determine not to let self-pity be your friend anymore. It is not too much for you. If you kick out every lie, I believe you will come out the other side with new strength and maturity.

## LIE NUMBER TWO: "NOTHING EVER GOES RIGHT FOR ME!"

Some apparently understandable beliefs are just plain wrong. Although this one is common, it is always untrue. Proverbs 23:7 teaches, "For as he thinks in his heart, so is he..." What we meditate on affects our lives. A verse later on in the same chapter adds that your "expectation shall not be cut off." (Proverbs 23:18 KJV). In other words, we become what we think and we get what we expect. When we listen to the lie that nothing ever works out, we end up opening the door to failure. Our inner beliefs create an atmosphere of doubt and fear which the enemy exploits.

This thought is not only unhelpful, it is also always untrue. Some things must have worked out for you. Your car started, or your train came. You had the money to buy this book, or maybe it was a gift. You can read, so someone educated you. You can think, therefore your brain is functioning. You can breathe which means your lungs are working.

In the midst of tragedy, the enemy wants us to look at our lives through grey-tinted glasses. Self-pity wants you to see pain and strain everywhere you look. In fact, it is immensely helpful to see the good in our lives, especially when some things have gone wrong. This lie is very similar to another one: "I have messed everything up!" Apply the same principles. You may have made a major mistake at work, but you have not messed everything up in your life. You can still drive, you can still breathe, you can still believe God to turn everything around for good (see Romans 8:28). He is able. Whatever lie you have been listening to, you will eventually find it satisfying to challenge thoughts you once blindly accepted. The first step is noticing the barrage of unhelpful ideas that whir around your mind. Once you become conscious of false thinking, you can kick it out.

# BREAKING FREE

Fiona contended with more than her fair share of hardship. Abused for more than a decade by her grandfather, father, aunt, cousin and a neighbor, she felt like a slab of meat that meant nothing to anyone. For many years, anger raged and she lashed out at anyone who seemed to care. She also struggled daily with suicidal thoughts. Fiona came to our two day conference several times as she allowed God to heal her shattered heart. Once numb and detached, this precious young woman began to feel again.

As the pain gradually drained away, Fiona's life started to improve. However, years of abuse and betrayal left her feeling like a victim. She anticipated disappointment and expected to be rejected. She believed that nothing would ever go well. As she took hold of the principles I've included in this book, she began to look for the good around her. I will never forget the day when she contacted us to share her breakthrough: "As I waited for my ride to arrive, gratitude arose and I began to acknowledge how blessed I was to have a job and a future. It was like something bad snapped off me that day. It was my new beginning!" Fiona refused to entertain the lie that nothing ever went right in her life and instead started to see the good around her. It might not sound like a huge breakthrough, but it sparked her new start.

# LIE NUMBER THREE: "IT SHOULD BE GOOD!"

Another lie that the enemy throws at us is that if we are in the center of God's will, life should be good. This is wrong and unhelpful. Psalms 34:19 says, "Many are the afflictions of the righteous, but the Lord delivers him out of them all." The Hebrew word for afflictions is *ra* and it means adversity, calamity, distress and misery. The Bible is telling us that we will experience difficult seasons, but that whatever we go through, the Lord will provide a way out. If we believe the lie that believers should not face problems, we will probably feel short changed by life's letdowns.

1 Peter 4:12-13 (NLT) is clear: "Dear friends, don't be surprised at the fiery trials you are going through, as if something strange were happening to you. Instead, be very glad—for these trials make you partners with Christ in his suffering, so that you will have the wonderful joy of seeing his glory when it is revealed to all the world." I encourage you to reset your mindset. Recognize that times of trouble are part of life, but also acknowledge that you have the strength to endure because Jesus is in your corner.

## LIE NUMBER FOUR: "THE WORLD REVOLVES AROUND ME"

There is a line in a song by the rock group U2 that goes, "When I was three, I thought the world revolved around me. I was wrong." If only we all grew out of this idea by the time we were four years old! Self-absorption is awful for everyone. Being preoccupied with ourselves does not feel good. It drains our energy and it is unpleasant for other people.

Proverbs 30:15-16 says, 'The leech has two daughters—Give and Give! There are three things that are never satisfied, four never say, "Enough!": The grave, The barren womb, The earth that is not satisfied with water—And the fire never says, "Enough!"' Let's start at the beginning of this verse. When we are the center of our attention, we can become like that leech which is always asking for something from someone. This verse then makes the connection between constant requests and the inability to be satisfied. When we are self-absorbed, we will never be content. The less we focus on ourselves, the more enjoyable our lives will become.

Society tells us that we must look out for number one. "If I don't look out for myself," so the story goes, "...no one else will." The importance of keeping self at the center is one of the lies pedaled by our pretend friend. However, 2 Timothy 3:1-2 (AMPC) lays out the truth: "But understand this, that in the last days will come (set in) perilous times of great stress and trouble [hard to deal with and hard to bear]. For people will be lovers of self and [utterly] self-centered..." Self-pity keeps our eyes on our own lives. It tells us that self-centeredness is the right response to stress and trouble. However, this just digs us even deeper into the pain of life's pressures.

Focusing on self when times are tough makes us feel worse. Whatever we meditate on grows in our minds. Remember that Proverbs 23:7 tells us that we become what we think about. The more we dwell on the misery of our own lives, the more that misery can intensify. In contrast, thinking about others takes our eyes off our misery and dilutes the pain. Eventually, focusing on someone else will make your life more enjoyable.

## POOR ME 'PRAYERS'

Self-pity can even infect our prayer life. Let me explain using the story of the Red Sea crossing. Soon after letting the Israelites go, the Egyptian taskmasters regretted releasing their former slaves. The Egyptians gathered an army and chased after them. When the Israelites turned to see their oppressors in pursuit, their joy and faith quickly turned to terror: '...They cried out to the Lord and they said to Moses, "Why did you bring us out here to die in the wilderness? ... What have you done to us? Why did you make us leave Egypt?"' (Exodus 14:10b-11 NLT)

All sorts of emotions were released. Not only were they afraid, they felt let down and blamed their leader for their mess. Let's look at God's answer to Moses for the children of Israel: "Why are you crying out to me? Tell the people to get moving!" (Exodus 14:15). God shut down their whining and instead asked them to get going. His heart is to help us, but when we are consumed with self-pity we may just be delaying His intervention.

Years ago, I attended a huge conference by myself. As I arrived, I was shown to a seat on the front row. I happened to be wearing an unusual canary yellow top. As I sat down, I looked around to see that someone right behind me had the exact same top. If you're a woman, you may already be feeling my pain, but my 'twin' happened to be about twelve years of age! I could not believe my misfortune.

## GET ME OUT OF HERE!

Just then the next speaker began his session. He opened with a very accurate prophetic word for a woman high up in the rafters. The television cameras eventually found her and soon a lady's face was being broadcast on giant screens all around the auditorium. As I looked up, I was stunned. She was also wearing the exact same canary yellow top! I was on my own, embarrassed and feeling exceptionally sorry for myself.

Sitting down, I shut my eyes and prayed, "God, this is awful. I feel so stupid. Please get me out of here!" I was stunned by the Lord's immediate answer. He didn't reassure me of His wonderful love and comfort me. He spoke firmly to my spirit: "I don't want to hear your self-pity. I want to hear your faith." God was not moved by my "poor me" prayers! I'm not even sure that He was paying attention to my words. He wanted me to grow up and get over myself. Whatever situation we are in, the Lord is always listening for faith because that is what enables Him to act on our behalf.

I encourage you to pay attention to the tone of your prayers. Are they filled with faith or self-pity? Do you remind the Lord of His faithfulness or cry out in anguish, telling Him you can't wait any longer? Do you tell Him it's all too much or declare His promises over your life? Of course we need to be real with our Heavenly Father and pour out pain in His presence. However, we do not need to tolerate self-absorbed pity-me prayers. They won't make anything better and they may even delay our breakthrough.

## PLEASE, PLEASE PRAY...

It is amazing how often self-pity asks others to pray. I can't tell you how many times I have contacted my prayer partner and pleaded, "Please, please pray!" It is great to share our needs with our nearest and dearest. That is not the same as begging others for their sympathy prayers. That is exactly what I did when I felt badly done by. I wanted others to stand in *my* gap.

Ezekiel 22:30 says, "So I sought for a man among them who would... stand in the gap before Me on behalf of the land..." The Bible asks us to stand in the gap and pray for those who *cannot* pray for themselves. There are some conflicts that we must tackle in agreement with others. Other battles you and I can fight alone. We should rarely ask others to pray for our breakthrough when we are not willing. All too often, that is the way we behave when we are feeling sorry for ourselves.

I love the story that an American pastor once told. A lady in his church used to come at the end of every service and ask him to intercede for her. After a while, this pastor got fed up of her constant requests. He had a big congregation and yet she wanted him to focus all his prayer time on her. One Sunday, she made her way to the front as usual and whimpered, "Pastor, pray for me." He retorted curtly, "Aaah, pray for yourself!" I think I probably deserved this response to my requests for prayer from time to time! Let's pray for ourselves, right now.

**Heavenly Father,**

I realize how many lies I have believed. Please forgive me. I ask You to help me to dismantle any mindset that has been built on these false beliefs. (*Now tell the Lord exactly which lies you believed. Explain how they impacted your life and ask Him to forgive you for every wrong view.*) Thank You, Lord, for the power of Your Word. Please help me to be aware of any lies that come into my mind. When I realize I am thinking something wrong, I will, "...take captive every thought to make it obedient to Christ." (2 Corinthians 10:5 NIV). I choose to replace every lie I have believed with the truth.

I renounce self-absorption from my life and prayers. I ask for Your help to take my eyes off my own life. I choose to reset my mindset and declare that I will be transformed by changing the way I think (see Romans 12:2). I ask for Your daily help to renew my mind and I thank You for the joy and freedom that await me.

In Jesus' name I pray,

Amen.

**If you realize that lies have been central to your thinking, please pray with me:**

In the name of Jesus, I dismantle every demonic stronghold that I have built in my mind. I destroy every lie that held me bound in Jesus' name. (*Deal with any major lies one by one and explain exactly how those lies were framed in your thoughts.*) Holy Spirit, please reveal the truth of Your Word to my heart concerning these lies. I will build my life upon Your Word and Your truth from this day forward.

In Jesus' name,

Amen.

# Chapter 7

# ISOLATION

Right at the start, God looked at His creation and reached a conclusion: "It is not good that man should be alone..." (Genesis 2:18). You and I were made for fellowship. We were designed to enjoy all sorts of different relationships. In fact, we cannot experience the abundant life that Jesus died to give us while we keep others at arm's length. But that's not all. Being connected with the right people actually enables us to fulfill our God-given purpose. Let's look at some destiny connections in Scripture that illustrate our need for one another.

Abraham could not become the father of faith without Sarah and Lot prospered as long as he was with Abraham. Jacob relied upon the help of Leah, Rachel (and their respective assistants) to birth a nation. Joseph needed a butler and his boss Pharaoh to become the savior of two nations. Moses depended upon the wise advice of his father-in-law to enable him to lead Israel in the wilderness. Elisha learned from Elijah. King David relied upon Jonathan for protection. Esther carefully followed Mordecai's instructions to become queen and then save the entire Jewish race. I could go on. Just as our Bible heroes needed others to achieve their potential, so you and I need our destiny partners. That is one reason why the enemy sorely tempts us to separate ourselves.

# WHEN LIFE THROWS CURVEBALLS

As a teenager, Madeline suffered from serious anemia. She had headaches, frequent dizzy spells and lacked energy. After being referred to her local hospital in her home country of South Africa, she was given repeated blood transfusions. However, months of painful procedures proved to be pointless: the treatment was unsuccessful. Doctors went on to prescribe iron tablets (which should have been their first defense against anemia). Within a matter of weeks, Madeline was well.

Fast forward ten years... Madeline moved to the UK, married and started a family. When her daughter was just two weeks old, she became seriously ill. At first, doctors weren't sure what was wrong so they ran numerous tests. Madeline will never forget the day that doctors called her into a consultation room to tell her that her princess was HIV positive. This diagnosis inevitably led to more tests and soon Madeline was informed that she was the one who had infected her child. Unnecessary blood transfusions when she was a teenager led to both mother and child being HIV positive.

Treatment back then for HIV was limited and the newspapers were filled with tragic stories of people dying of AIDS. This news was therefore soul-destroying. Not only was life expectancy for both mom and child cut short, Madeleine was also told that she must not have any other children. "This was the final straw," Madeline explained. "I was devastated. As one of seven children, my desire since childhood was to have a big family of my own. In one conversation, all my dreams were dashed. I felt like a failure. I no longer believed I was good enough for my husband: he deserved a real woman who could give him a family. I didn't know how long my daughter and I would live. I was angry and I lost hope. Self-pity gripped me. I shut down inside and shut the world out."

# SEEING THE END OF THE TUNNEL

The injustice of the situation taunted this precious South African lady. Madeline listened to self-pity's lies that no one could understand her pain and isolated herself. She continued attending church and went through the motions of Christian living, yet was silently nursing her wounds. A couple of years passed. However, in many ways, life stood still for Madeline. That was until she began a deep healing journey. Through our healing events, the Lord started to shine His light into the depths of her heart. She released the anger and injustice and was restored. Then God started to show Madeline that she had become a victim of self-pity.

"I felt God asking me to stop blaming other people for the state of my life," Madeline explained. "It was terribly painful at first. After holding others responsible for my misery, it was hard to let that go. But in the end, it felt liberating to take back control of my destiny. I realized that I was blessed. Instead of grumbling, gratitude started to well up inside. It was amazing." The relief she felt when she walked away from self-pity was wonderful. As medicine advanced, Madeline went on to have three more children who are all completely healthy. In addition, she and her firstborn are better than ever. Perhaps equally as important, Madeline is a now generous and selfless minister being used by God to bring healing to the hearts of men and women around the world.

# A DEMONIC PLOT

The enemy wants to isolate you and me. He wants to separate us from the people who God placed in our lives. Sometimes he does that physically: he sows seeds of discontent or mistrust in our hearts so we walk away from destiny relationships. At other times, the devil tempts us to shut down emotionally. We may be surrounded by people, but living behind huge walls we built around our hearts. In Psalms 94:17, the Psalmist made an insightful statement: "Unless the Lord had been my help, my soul would soon have settled in silence." Shutdown is not God's will for anyone. We were made in the image of God and we were designed for fellowship. He places the lonely in families (Psalm 68:6) because seclusion is ultimately destructive.

Jesus told Peter that He had prayed for him. Through intercession, the Lord destroyed the enemy's plan: 'And the Lord said, "Simon, Simon! Indeed, Satan has asked for you, that he may sift you as wheat."' (Luke 22:31) When you sift, you separate one substance from another. The devil wanted to separate Peter from the other disciples. He knew that the apostles needed one another to fulfill both their individual callings and their collective mission. That was the Lord's divine design.

Let me explain. The God of heaven and earth chose to make Himself reliant upon the people He created to fulfill His purposes. Psalms 115:16 (AMPC) is clear: "The heavens are the Lord's heavens, but the earth has He given to the children of men." God needs you and me to fulfill His plans on earth. In the same way, you and I need one another to achieve our highest potential. We cannot succeed without divine relationships. That is the way God made us. No one person has all the gifts or all the answers. We need one another to thrive. Our pretend friend knows this, so he tempts us to pull away from pivotal people. Self-pity wants you to close your heart to particular friends or family and shut down inside. We must fight back by renouncing the use of silence as a weapon.

## SAVED FROM THE SIFTING

On resurrection Sunday, an angel appeared to Mary Magdalene, Mary the mother of James, and Salome. After sharing the extraordinary news that Jesus was alive, the angel said these exact words to the ladies, "But go, tell His disciples—and Peter—that He is going before you into Galilee; there you will see Him, as He said to you." (Mark 16:7). The angel told the women to give this news to the disciples *and* Peter. The plan of the enemy was already unfolding. Satan was separating Peter from his friends in an attempt to separate Peter from his destiny. The one who was once at the center of the twelve was now on the outside.

Peter may have believed that he had permanently disqualified himself from his destiny. Despite being warned that he would deny the Lord, he still went ahead and told three different people that he did not know Jesus. Perhaps he was beating himself up for his disloyalty. He could have been overwhelmed with shame. It might not be surprising that Peter isolated himself, but that does not make it even slightly right. Thank God that Jesus' prayers and this angelic intervention foiled a demonic plot. The women shared the great news of Jesus with Peter (as well as the disciples) and he was reunited with his destiny friends.

## WHAT'S THE ENEMY'S PURPOSE?

Our pretend friend tells us that we are right to listen to his lies. We isolate ourselves, we are told, for our own protection. No one else cares the way they should, we are persuaded. This is fiction. Proverbs 18:1 (AMPC) says, "He who willfully separates and estranges himself [from God and man] seeks his own desire and pretext to break out against all wise and sound judgment."

The first lesson we learn from this scripture is that pushing people away also shuts God out. It is the Lord who put people in our lives in the first place. He placed us in relationships so we can grow and share. God is not the author of problems so it was never His will that we would be wounded or betrayed. We need to be healed when we are hurt. The remedy is never isolation.

Secondly, this scripture teaches us that separation serves self. "He who separates himself... seeks his own desire..." When I shut down inside, I am not doing it to protect other people. I am thinking about myself. The Hebrew word for desire in this verse is ta'ăwâ and it means satisfaction. When we pull away, we are satisfying ourselves. We are looking out for number one. The tendency to retreat is not only destructive, but selfish.

I love the use of the word *pretext* in the amplified version of this verse. Let's look at it again: "He who willfully separates and estranges himself [from God and man] seeks his own desire and *pretext* to break out against all wise and sound judgment." (Proverbs 18:1 AMPC). The dictionary definition of pretext is, *'something that is put forward to conceal a true purpose.'* The third lesson from this verse is that isolation is a way of avoiding the counsel and wisdom of others. That might sound harsh. However, we need to remember that we often don't know what is really going on inside until God's Word exposes it.

## UNCOVERING THE ENEMY

Jeremiah 17:9 (AMPC) says, "The heart is deceitful above all things... Who can know it [perceive, understand, be acquainted with his own heart and mind]?" I cannot tell you how many times the Holy Spirit has shown me my true motives. The truth is often painful, but it is always liberating. When you and I separate ourselves, we unwittingly push God away. We are being self-centered and we are avoiding correction. No wonder the devil works hard to disconnect us from our destiny friends.

Proverbs 13:20 says, "He who walks with wise men will be wise..." Becoming wise usually requires effort. We are told to expand our knowledge, pray for wisdom, confess that wisdom is our sister and much more. However, Proverbs 13:20 teaches that just by hanging out with great men and women, we will grow! It should not be surprising that the enemy relentlessly seeks to separate us from our most influential relationships.

## WHEN IT'S REALLY NOT WHAT WE WANT

Isolation is not always a choice. Perhaps you have no family or few friends. Feeling alone can produce a deafening silence. Walking through the door that was once shared with someone special. Sitting by yourself with a knot in your stomach. Loneliness can feel like a cold cloak separating you from companionship and love. Maybe you have people around you, but you still feel a deep, unmet need for companionship. Perhaps you can't relate to others. You might be unable to share your thoughts and feelings freely. An unloving marriage can be a desolate place. People assume you have it all, but you feel empty and alone. You long for intimacy, looking back with longing at the times when you shared so much. Now, you may feel like you are just sharing a house with a fellow tenant.

I remember being on my own at a conference. During the lunch for special guests, ministers dined with their travel companions while I sat by myself at a table for two. No one did anything to wound me and yet I felt hurt by the isolation. I looked around, pretending to be searching for someone when really I was looking for anyone. Loneliness can feel like rejection. David experienced that at times: "Turn to me and be gracious to me, for I am lonely..." (Psalm 25:16). He was crying out to God saying, "I feel completely alone and it hurts!" Nearly every step of his journey, the king was surrounded by people and yet he felt lonely. Loneliness isn't always a lack of relationships. Often it is an issue of the heart.

# COMING OUT

A wonderful man called Tom came to one of our two day Healed for Life conferences. He was 74 years of age and had suffered a great deal throughout his life. Every session God did something new in his heart. He was healed of the lasting wounds of bullying at school, as well as years of rejection by family members. I will never forget his testimony several months later: "God shone His light into my heart. He healed hidden hurts that I had no idea were still holding me back. But it was not until I got home that I realized what the Lord had really done. After a lifetime of loneliness, I now feel surrounded by love and fellowship. My circumstances haven't changed, but my heart has been healed of loneliness." Many people wept as he shared his story. If you are lonely, then I would love to lead you in prayer before we go any further:

**Heavenly Father,**

I ask for your help: I feel very alone and it hurts. I ask You to heal me of every inner sense of loneliness. It makes me feel rejected deep down. (*Now tell the Lord in as much detail as possibly exactly how you feel and what makes you feel that way.*) I ask You to reach into my heart and take this pain away. I give it to You, knowing that You are my friend and Comforter.

I also ask You to bring two or three destiny friends into my life. I know that You want me to enjoy fellowship so I open my heart to the right people. Thank You that You care about every aspect of my life.

In Jesus' name I pray,

Amen.

# VICIOUS CYCLES

The enemy really plays games with us. One of the rotten fruits of loneliness is self-pity. And self-pity makes us retreat into solitude where we feel all the more alone. Our pretend friend always targets those who feel isolated with sadness and lies. This makes an already difficult situation worse. If you are suffering from loneliness, God wants to heal your heart. He longs to take your pain away and bring lasting restoration. Use the chapter in the next section to help you to continue pouring out any pain in His presence. As you do, He will pour in His liquid love. The best relationships are divinely orchestrated, so I am believing with you that God will knit you together with friends who will help you fulfill your purpose. He is faithful. He knows you better than you know yourself and understands how to meet your deepest needs.

There is an inner resilience that arises when we are healed. Psalm 27:14 says, "He shall strengthen your heart..." When I first started travelling to the United States, I was worried about being alone. Ten hour flights followed by empty hotel rooms sounded scary. I was concerned that my husband and children would feel very far away. Self-pity was trying to set in before I even stepped out of the house! I went to my Heavenly Father in prayer, told Him how I felt and asked Him to strengthen me. God is so kind. He didn't just make me more robust. He revealed Himself to me as my closest companion, closer than any earthly friend. Now I love being by myself. Although I enjoy travelling with companions, I treasure time alone.

# ATTENTION

Self-pity craves attention. Sometimes it runs away and shuts the door to make people seek it out. At other times, it uses sickness or sad stories to attract attention. Dare I suggest that our pretend friend has even mastered social media as a way of gaining sympathy or compliments? For years, I was an attention-seeker. The truth is that our moment in the spotlight only temporarily fills the inner void. Then the emptiness returns. Attention will never create lasting satisfaction or security. We need to recognize any behavior which is designed to attract attention. We need to repent and then ask God's unchanging love to heal our hearts.

# DANGEROUS WAYS

We studied the story of the end of Elijah's ministry in chapter two. Exhaustion opened the door to self-pity, but it was when the prophet isolated himself that he started on a downward spiral. While we remain connected, the Lord can send an encourager. However, when we shut the world out, it becomes hard for us to receive from anyone. Let's look again at Proverbs 18:1 (AMPC): "He who willfully separates and estranges himself [from God and man] seeks his own desire and pretext to break out against all wise and sound judgment." This verse exposes our propensity to become stubborn when we isolate ourselves. We can end up actually resisting help.

The Lord visited Elijah in an amazing way in the cave where he was hiding, but the prophet was unmoved. He was listening to the enemy's lies instead of rising up again in gratitude. Isolating himself may well have been the final step that took Elijah out of the purposes of God. If this had the capacity to derail such a mighty man of God, then we probably need to guard our hearts. Let's pray.

**Heavenly Father,**

There are times when I have pushed people away and shut down inside. I now realize that this was wrong. I probably hurt others and I almost certainly harmed myself. I ask for Your forgiveness,

Lord. I break down any inner wall that I have built to protect myself. Proverbs 28:26 says that he who trusts in his own heart is a fool. I realize that I was trusting myself instead of You. Forgive me, Lord. I ask for the help and humility to rebuild destiny relationships. I will open my heart to the people that You have placed in my life. Help me to be wise in all my relationships. Thank You that by helping one another, we will fulfill our potential.

I renounce the use of silence as a weapon. I ask You to clean that dwelling place in my heart which was once a home to self-pity where demons felt comfortable. Cleanse me, I pray, and fill me with Your wonderful love.

In Jesus' name, I pray,

Amen.

# Part Three

# REMEDIES

We can kick our pretend friend out of our lives. We do not need to be brought low by its lies or imprisoned by isolation. We can be completely free. In this section, we look at three remedies that will enable you to eradicate self-pity from your life.

# Chapter 8

# HEALING

Sexual abuse throughout Josh's childhood beat every shred of self-worth out of him. He hardened his heart and grew into an angry adult who was filled with self-pity. He treated his wife with contempt and his children were afraid of his frequent outbursts. Josh behaved as though the world owed him something. It was unpleasant for everyone. When Josh was thirty-five, he came to one of our conferences. As the Holy Spirit's love filled the room, Josh faced pain that had been trapped inside for decades. He told the Lord (and a member of our team) what had happened to him when he was young. Then he broke down and wept. This marked the start of an incredible journey to healing, but it also paved the way for Josh to kick self-pity out of his life. As he was restored, he began to understand his worth. Eventually, healing and gratitude drove our pretend friend out of his life. Josh is now a wonderful family man who lives to see others set free from pain and anguish.

## A UNIVERSAL NEED

We all get wounded in life. You may have been betrayed by someone you trusted. You could have lost someone you dearly loved. Perhaps your lifelong dreams crashed down around you. It may not be as dramatic as that. Things may have been said that crushed your confidence or pierced your heart. Delays to all-important breakthroughs might have made you feel forgotten. You could have been rejected, ridiculed or overlooked at work. It is impossible to avoid getting hurt. But what do we do about it? Most of the time, we just dust ourselves off and then carry on as best we can. All too often, we end up feeling deflated or discouraged. We may avoid situations that could cause further hurt. Your heart may become heavy.

King David suffered in many ways throughout his life. In Psalms 27:10 (AMPC), David wrote, "... my father and my mother have forsaken me..." so he knew the pain of being abandoned by his parents. Although he knew his dad Jesse, there is no sign of his mom ever being a part of his life. From his teenage years, he was ridiculed by his brothers. Later on, he was rejected by them (see 1 Samuel 17:28 and Psalm 69:8). King Saul took David under his wing and the young warrior saw him as a spiritual father. However, just a couple of years later, Saul turned on David and his affection for the shepherd boy turned to hatred. The king no longer nurtured our hero, but instead instructed his soldiers to hunt him down. After David was crowned king, both his own son Absalom and a leader called Sheba tried to steal the kingdom from him. This man suffered a great deal and was often heartbroken by the way he was treated.

## THE REAL DEAL

We can learn a lot from the one that God called "... a man after My own heart." (1 Samuel 13:14). Sometimes we assume that we need to be super-spiritual to please the Lord. But David's relationship with Yahweh was real. Not only did he praise God in hard times, he also brought his difficulties and disappointments to Him in prayer. He understood the power of coming to the Lord as his wonderful counsellor (see Isaiah 9:6). Indeed, we can read many examples of King David telling his Heavenly Father about his sadness and pain in detail. In Psalms 62:8 (AMPC), David encourages the people to follow in his footsteps: "Trust in, lean on, rely on, and have confidence in Him at all times, you people; pour out your hearts before Him. God is a refuge for us (a fortress and a high tower). Selah [pause, and calmly think of that]!"

Listen to the way that David poured out his disappointment before the Lord in Psalms 55:12-13 (NLT) "It is not an enemy who taunts me—I could bear that. It is not my foes who so arrogantly insult me—I could have hidden from them. Instead, it is you—my equal, my companion and close friend." David did not restrict his prayer life to spiritual matters. David told the Lord about his heartbreak and explained exactly how he had been hurt. It is this same David who God said was a man after His own heart. The Lord wants us to share our pain with Him. Just as you probably appreciate it when someone you love shares their heart with you, so our Heavenly Father is glad when we pour out our pain in His presence.

## DIVINE DESIGN

Your soul was made for the giving and receiving of love. It was made for fellowship. Your heart was not designed to house pain. The Lord therefore created a release mechanism called tears. Just as a healthy body emits toxins via urine, so a healthy soul releases pain by weeping. When our tears are directed correctly, they unleash restoration. Just crying will not normally bring lasting relief. Many people weep out of frustration or hurt without getting healed. However, when we learn how to pour out our hearts before the face of the Lord, we will be made whole. I have had the privilege of leading countless people across the world to restoration. Men and women who have been abused, betrayed or bereaved have been made whole when they have released their pain in the presence of God.

There is a big difference between the occasional tear and pouring out pain. I often see people working hard to constrain their pain, trying to cry politely. In Psalm 18:6, David said, "I cried out to You in my distress... and... you heard my troubled cry. My sobs came right into Your heart and You turned Your face to rescue me." (TPT). Crying *out* is not the same as crying. When we cry out, there is a thrust behind our tears and agony leaves. Crying is simply tears falling.

Picture a bottle of soda pop that has been shaken. The bottle represents your soul and the shaken pop your pain. If you slightly unscrew the lid, liquid will spill out, but you can never empty a bottle that way. To get it all out, you need to take off the lid and pour it. Crying is like spilling. Crying *out* is like pouring. Another important point is that weeping is not the same as weeping in the presence of God. David said, "I cry out to You..." I can weep all night long without any relief if I am doing so alone. When I pour out my pain before the Lord, I am bringing my broken heart to Him for healing. David sobbed on God, the Lord turned His face towards His precious son and rescued him from his pain.

## STRONG MEN CRY

Adults often tell children to dry their eyes. Crying is seen by some as soft. There is a popular myth that *real men don't cry*. This is simply not true. Any culture which teaches that weeping is weakness is wrong. Joseph, one of the Bible's greatest leaders, sobbed in public on several occasions. Not once did he seem ashamed or embarrassed. In fact, he cried freely and frequently - even though he was the second most powerful man in the land. It is not only Joseph who knew how to weep. We have countless biblical examples of mighty men pouring out their hearts, both in private and public.

In Psalms 6:6 (NLT), King David said, "I am worn out from sobbing. All night I flood my bed with weeping, drenching it with my tears." Did you catch that? This mighty warrior soaked his bed with tears as he recounted every agonizing trial to the Lord in prayer. Jeremiah, who was known as the weeping prophet, cried before God and he encouraged the people of Israel to do the same: "... Pour out your heart like water before the face of the Lord..." (Lamentations 2:19). The Apostle Paul shed tears freely and the Ephesian elders sobbed when they said goodbye to their leader (Acts 20:37). And our greatest example, Jesus, wept too (John 11:35).

The strongest (and probably the largest) member of our church is a weights trainer, ironically known as Junior. He was raised in terrible poverty during the civil war in Sierra Leone. Junior went hungry and had to wear shoes made of wire. He was nearly killed as a teenager on three separate occasions and witnessed atrocities no one should have to see. After escaping to the UK, the Lord gloriously saved and then healed Junior. This loving husband and father is now one of the biggest softies I know! When the presence of the Lord visits a meeting, he is one of the first to fall to his knees and worship, tears streaming down his face.

My husband and I love to watch movies together. If a film is about human tragedy, it is not uncommon for both of us to sob. Schindler's List is the remarkable story of a hero who helped save hundreds of Jews in Nazi Germany. After we watched the movie, we both wept for about ten minutes. While I weep during a film about human turmoil, I often find myself praying that the Lord will increase my compassion for the crushed. I always ask for a greater anointing to bring healing to the hurting. On those occasions, my tears release a deeper love for those who desperately need God's help.

# THE KEY THAT UNLOCKS THE DOOR

Pain is usually bound up by words. Let's go back to the analogy of a bottle of soda pop. For the purposes of illustration, the lid represents our words. When the top is unscrewed and removed, the liquid can be poured out. When something horrible happens, there are usually things that we need to say in order to release the pain. Trapped words in turn will trap pain. When we say exactly what hurt us, pain can be released and tears usually flow.

Kate, who had been repeatedly abused by church leaders, came to Healed for Life. On arrival, she explained that she was totally detached from her emotions. She knew she needed healing, but could not feel her pain. Prompted by the Holy Spirit, one of our team led Kate in prayer to say what she had never said. Kate blurted out the words, "It was SO VERY WRONG!" Suddenly, a torrent of pain flooded out of her soul. She fell to the floor and wept for the first time in many years while the Lord healed her heart. Unspoken words needed to be said for Kate's pain to be released.

Our hearts are like houses with twisting corridors leading to different rooms. When something hurtful happens, it is as though a room inside our soul gets blocked with pain. The way to unlock the door to that room is by returning to the memory in the presence of God and saying what we never said. When we tell the Lord exactly what we went through and how much it hurt, we release the sorrow. Healing tears can then flow. Lamentations 2:19 says, "Pour out your heart like water before the face of the Lord." When we pour out our hearts, we share the most intimate details of our lives with someone we trust.

# OUR WONDERFUL COUNSELOR

Jesus is called our Wonderful Counselor (Isaiah 9:6). Counseling works when a client shares their memories (and the feelings associated with them) with their counselor. Jesus is not a mere man. He is our wonderful, supernatural counselor. We need to talk to Him about every difficult detail of our lives. We need to share honestly about how the events of our lives made us feel. When we pour out our hearts before Him, He releases His healing love into our lives.

After our daughter Naomi died, I told my Heavenly Father how much I missed my little girl and how empty I felt without her. I told Him that I ached inside and could not stand the agony. I wept loudly and frequently as I shared my sadness with the Lord. I made a decision that the grief was better out than in.

Even at work, I made an agreement with my boss to ensure I could release pain when necessary. Whenever I said, "Back in five," he knew what to expect. I would leave the room immediately (with no one following me) and take refuge in a deserted corridor where I would cry. After powdering my nose, I would return to my desk and continue my work. I maintained my professionalism, but not at the expense of my emotional well-being.

In the months after Naomi died, I poured out a great deal of pain in God's presence. Bit by bit, my Heavenly Father healed my broken heart. My journey to restoration was made up of a mixture of outpourings in prayer and supernatural healing encounters.

From reading the book of Genesis, I am convinced that Joseph learned how to give his anguish to God through years of suffering and disappointment. The Bible records seven different occasions when Joseph wept. He cried loudly, with tears streaming down his face. He wept alone, he wept in front of his brothers and he wept as he hugged his father for the first time since their separation. He knew how to be made whole by pouring out his heart. Let's create a new culture where releasing our emotions in a healthy manner is not only acceptable, but celebrated.

# THE POWER OF ENCOUNTERS

About a month after Naomi died, I decided it was time to tidy away her toys. As I packed away her favorite playthings, pain overwhelmed me. Not knowing how to hold myself together, I cried out to God from the depths of my being: "Help!" Almost immediately, I felt a hand reach down from heaven and into my heart. My Heavenly Father pulled out my pain. Within a matter of minutes, the agony of that moment was over. I sat on my sofa exhausted and yet astonished at God's supernatural healing power.

That is just one example of many healing encounters I experienced in the presence of the Lord. Today, I can talk about our first daughter with great love, but no sorrow. Her birthdays and anniversaries come and go without any sadness. My husband and I are completely healed. Depending on the circumstances of your journey through life, you may need repeated healing experiences. Just as we may have to go to the doctor on several occasions for certain conditions, so we might need repeated visits to our Heavenly Healer.

# THE OVERFLOW

Restoration never stops with us. God did not only mend my heart. He turned my river of pain into a spring of healing. Every time my team and I minister, people are restored. The Holy Spirit shines His light into the depths of people's souls. He reveals hidden hurt and then He heals. God sets people free from inner issues they did not even know were hampering their lives. They leave our events refreshed, energized and ready to live life to the full. What He did for me, He will do for you.

2 Corinthians 1:3-4 (NLT) says, "All praise to God, the Father of our Lord Jesus Christ. God is our merciful Father and the source of all comfort. He comforts us in all our troubles so that we can

comfort others. When they are troubled, we will be able to give them the same comfort God has given us." Our Heavenly Father longs to heal every hurt that is hindering your life. He seeks to remove every ounce of sadness on the inside. He will then fill you anew with His Spirit and anoint you to bring that same restoration and refreshment to others. It is a kick in the teeth to the devil every time one of God's children is restored. It adds insult to satan's injury when we go a step further and allow ourselves to become a vessel of healing for others.

# SPIRITUAL HEART SURGERY

Jack had been in ministry for twenty years when he came to Healed for Life. He booked because someone asked him, not because he thought he needed to receive. He had no idea that he was carrying so many burdens. Jack was overwhelmed by the depth of God's work within: "There are no words to describe what happened at Healed for Life. Since my early twenties, although I was serving God, I still felt incomplete. When things went wrong, all I could think about was all the other things that had gone wrong. I constantly sought validation for whatever I did. It seemed like I could never be satisfied with the compliments.

"The team at Healed for Life prayed for us during the ministry times and I walked away feeling completely free. It was as though I had been through spiritual open-heart surgery. I don't ever remember being this balanced and focused. For the first time in decades, everything is going in the right direction." When Jack returned home, his world changed. His family moved out of the hotel room where they had been staying and into their own home. Work opportunities opened up and he stepped into a brand new ministry. The Bible says in Proverbs 4:23 that our hearts determine the course of our lives. When we allow Him to heal us, we set ourselves up to succeed.

# GOD'S JOB

There is a clear division of responsibility between what God does and what you and I must do to pursue our healing journey. You don't need to engage in what many call navel-gazing. You don't need to dig around in the memories of the past. All you need to do is open your heart to the Holy Spirit and invite Him to begin a new work within. Proverbs 20:27 says, "The spirit of a man is the lamp of the Lord, searching all the inner depths of his heart." The Holy Spirit wants to search your heart for hidden hurts. As you open up your heart in prayer, He will reveal old wounds. You will probably then feel long forgotten pain. Finally, He will heal your soul. You will feel like you have been gently enveloped in the unconditional love of the Lord. Let's pray:

**Heavenly Father,**

Thank You for caring about every issue in my life. I ask You to search my heart and shine Your light into the depths of my soul. Reveal every inner issue that is holding me back and uncover unhealed hurts deep within. Where my emotions have been shut down, I ask You to open them up again. I ask You to heal me in any area where I need it so that I can be a channel of love and healing to others. Lead me on a journey to inner security and peace.

As you remain in the presence of the Lord, He will probably bring back painful memories. When that happens, tell the Lord what happened in as much detail as possible. Remember, He is your Wonderful Counselor and He cares about every detail of your life. Share exactly how you felt. If you were scared, tell Him, "Lord I was so scared. It was horrible. I didn't know what to do!" If you felt rejected, explain how that hurt you. For example, "What did I do wrong? Why did he leave? It wasn't fair. It made me feel like I wasn't enough..." Explain how you felt. When you feel like crying, cry out before the Lord. After you have talked to Him about your pain, pray the prayer that follows.

Heal my heart, I pray. Fill me with Your wonderful love, Lord. Pour out Your Spirit into my heart afresh. I declare that I am on the journey out of self-pity and into wholeness.

In Jesus' name,

Amen

# Chapter 9

# PERSPECTIVE

For years after my daughter died, I saw myself as a victim. When I stood at the school gates waiting for my son to finish lessons, I viewed myself as the bereaved mum. The one who had suffered the unimaginable agony of losing her child. Others had normal stories - or so I supposed. I saw myself as different from other people. Someone who had been to hell and back and come out alive. I was constantly aware of my back story.

One of the problems with self-pity is that our issues become the centerpiece of our lives. I genuinely believed that my lot in life was the worst. There is a scene in an old Irish sitcom featuring two priests. One is smart while the other is woefully slow. In one scene, the priests are looking at two cows. One is a small plastic toy and the other is a real cow across the valley. The slow priest suggested that the distant animal was a miniature! "No, Dougal," the smart priest says. "This one is small. That one is far away!"

This perfectly describes what happens in our hearts when self-pity has its way. Our perspective becomes distorted. Our trials and tragedies tower above the difficulties of others. We assume their issues are miniature in comparison. In reality, other people's problems are rarely smaller. They are just further away from our thoughts.

# THE LAW OF AVERAGES

Let me get back to pick-up time at my son's school. Hundreds of other mothers and fathers waited for their children each day. The law of averages means that I can make some assumptions about those parents' lives. Some will have been abused or molested as children by people they trusted. Others will have suffered the rejection and shame of marital unfaithfulness. A few will probably have been fighting terminal illness. Poverty, tragedy, agony and ruin are all around us. However, when our trauma is the focus of our world-view, we develop a distorted perspective that has 'me, myself and I' at the center.

Ecclesiastes 1:9 says: "That which has been is what will be, That which is done is what will be done, and there is nothing new under the sun." The New Living Translation puts it this way: "History merely repeats itself. It has all been done before. Nothing under the sun is truly new." Although each one of us is unique, the trials and tests that we face are not. There is nothing that I have gone through that is new. Countless couples across the world have lost children. Far too many have lost entire families. Whatever you have suffered, according to the Bible (and the obvious law of averages) someone else has known that pain and come out the other side strong.

History repeats itself. Every trial has been faced by others through the centuries. The devil wants to magnify the pain of our particular tests. The enemy likes it when we think our suffering makes us different, but this is not true. 1 Corinthians 10:13 (New Living Translation) says, "The temptations in your life are no different from what others experience...". The Greek word for temptation here is the same as the one for trial. The trials that you and I have experienced have been endured by many others the world over.

When we realize that our struggle is not all that different from the battles that others have had to fight, it can help us to put our lives into some sort of perspective. If we take our eyes off our individual circumstances and remember that suffering is all around us, we can start to have a more unselfish outlook. When we fix our eyes on Jesus who is able to bring us out of every and any trial, the Lord can start a new work within.

# ENTITLED

Self-pity makes us feel entitled. After my daughter died, I believed that I deserved extra compassion from the people around me. When times were tough, I expected special concessions. When I was behaving badly, I thought I should be excused of any guilt. After all, I was a bereaved mother. When life was good, I saw myself as a hero for being happy. I felt entitled to special treatment. I believed I should be handled differently. This even affected my relationship with the Lord. I expected God to answer my prayers because He owed me a consolation prize.

In Matthew 17:20b, Jesus said, 'If you have faith... you will say to this mountain, "Move from here to there," and it will move; and nothing will be impossible for you.' Scripture is clear. It is faith, not self-pity, that moves mountains. Remember, faith is of the heart (see Romans 10:10). If we want change in our lives, we will have to get back into faith. We need to empty our souls of self-pity so that we can fill our hearts with faith. The two cannot cohabit. Entitlement is based on what I think I deserve because of the story of my life. Faith is focused on the favor I enjoy because Jesus sacrificed His life. A sense of entitlement will never get us anything from God. Faith, on the other hand, pleases our Heavenly Father and will unlock heaven's blessings. Faith and self-pity will never be good bedfellows.

# MOMENTS OF TRUTH

I can point to several transformational moments in my life. The day that my English spiritual mom spoke the truth into my life was one. I tell the story in Lifting the Mask of Lois Gott leaning across a lunch table at a pastors' convention and saying: "The problem with you, Jo, is that it's all about position." I was stunned (and upset, if I am honest). I could have pushed back or become offended, but neither of those reactions would have helped me grow. Instead, I sat in silence.

Pastor Lois continued. "You have never faced some deep pain from your childhood." I debated with her for a while because I thought I was good. I had been through inner healing and assumed I was fine. Then suddenly, the Spirit of Truth pierced my defenses and I broke down and wept. For the first time in my life, the real condition of my heart was laid bare. In that moment, I realized that without my positions or job titles, and without my achievements or successes, I felt completely inadequate. As just Jo, I was not enough. I wept as God started to heal hurts that were buried in my heart. This encounter set my life on a new course. It was transformational.

An equally momentous occasion was when I accepted responsibility for my life. This time, no one spoke to me. No one challenged me. Something on the inside woke up and I knew I had to stop blaming people or circumstances for my lot. It was difficult, to say the least. I had spent a lifetime attributing my state of affairs to the actions of others. I now knew that my future depended upon me taking responsibility.

I realized that I was wholly responsible for my moods. I was accountable for my attitude at all times. I had to answer for the way I behaved. No more pointing to the past. No more excuses. I remember the first time my new outlook on life was tested. I was having lunch with a friend who asked me, "So what's your story?" In the past, that would have been my license to tell a string of anecdotes about how difficult my life had been. Instead, I replied quite simply, "There's not much to say. This is me."

## TURNING THE TIDE

My new outlook began to influence my relationships. An unexpected outcome was that I became less self-centered. The needs of others became more obvious. I no longer blamed my past for my present behavior - which was probably a relief to friends and family. Instead, I understood that my reactions were my responsibility. Although it was hard, it was also liberating. I took back control of my destiny.

If you have ever blamed your attitudes or actions on your lot in life, you have an opportunity. You too can take back control. You can walk away from any excuses you used to explain the way you are. You can start afresh. Romans 8:35 asks us an important question: "Who shall separate us from the love of Christ? Shall tribulation, or distress, or persecution, or famine, or nakedness, or peril, or sword?" Our trials cannot separate us from the love of the Lord, which is always enough to carry us through every season.

Paul the apostle learned to be content - and that means happy - even in dire circumstances. Philippians 4:11 (AMPC) says, "Not that I am implying that I was in any personal want, for I have learned how to be content (satisfied to the point where I am not disturbed or disquieted) in whatever state I am." So contentment is learned and it is also a choice. In reality, although breakthroughs give us a boost, they never create lasting happiness. While we try to find fulfillment from achievements of any kind, we will live in a state of frustration. True happiness is an inner atmosphere created by a combination of gratitude, peace and trust. Like the apostle, we get to choose our attitude and accepting responsibility is the first step towards a happier life.

## UNIMAGINABLE TRAUMA

There is a man who went through an unbelievable amount of suffering. He and his wife had a big family and were enjoying the blessings of God in virtually every area of life. They loved the Lord and served Him wholeheartedly. However, their children were all killed in a freak accident. I cannot imagine the pain of losing all your sons and daughters in one night. But that was their story. As if this wasn't enough, the man's highly successful business was destroyed around the same time. His wife turned against him and soon afterwards, he became terribly sick. Some of his friends tried to help, but in the end they only made things worse by spouting doctrine.

One whole book in the Old Testament describes the catastrophic events of this man's life and how he found his way out the other side. I believe his story is told to help us handle tragedy. There is much that we can learn from Job. He was a worshipper. When he didn't understand what was going on, he worshipped anyway. The day his children died, he did the unthinkable. He lifted up his eyes and praised. Job 1:20 records Job's reaction to this terrible tragedy: "Then Job arose, tore his robe, and shaved his head; and he fell to the ground and worshiped." He didn't deny his pain. When nothing made sense, he ran to God.

This grief-stricken father went through some serious lows in the seasons that followed. He regretted being born, became hopeless and was angry with everyone. I want us to fast forward to the last three chapters of the book. Job had thrown a host of accusations and questions at the Lord. Eventually, out of His immense love,

God answered Job. He did not enter into the rights and wrongs of what happened. He gave Job a fresh perspective. The Lord took Job's eyes off his life and turned his focus to the majesty of God. When we choose to dwell on the goodness of God, something changes inside.

# WHAT ABOUT THE CHILDREN?

Have you ever noticed that after Job's relationship with God was restored, the Lord gave him double of everything he lost? Job 1:3 says that at the outset: "his possessions were seven thousand sheep, three thousand camels, five hundred yoke of oxen, five hundred female donkeys..." By the end, he had double: "Now the Lord blessed the latter days of Job more than his beginning; for he had fourteen thousand sheep, six thousand camels, one thousand yoke of oxen, and one thousand female donkeys." (Job 42:12).

However, God did not give him double the number of children. Before tragedy hit Job's family, he had: "...seven sons and three daughters..." (Job 1:2). After the Lord's restoration, he had: "... seven sons and three daughters." (Job 42:13). Why would God place greater importance upon Job's animals than on his children? He gave Job double the livestock, but just 'replaced' his children. I remember the day I grappled with this issue.

While I was coming to terms with the loss of my daughter, I read this scripture and found it offensive if I am honest! That was until God revealed the real situation. I was reading with an earthly outlook while God only ever sees things from an eternal perspective. Job did not *lose* his children - they just moved location. God did give Job double. He had ten children waiting for him in heaven and ten with him on earth. Then, after what must have felt like the twinkling of an eye, he slipped into eternity - along with his huge family. It is helpful for you and I to see our lives from an eternal and not just an earthly perspective.

## HEAVENLY PERSPECTIVE

One of the things that troubled my husband and me after our daughter died was that she would miss us. It sounds very silly now, but back then we were concerned about her being all alone in heaven. Then my husband did the math. 2 Peter 3:8 says, "But, beloved, do not forget this one thing, that with the Lord one day is as a thousand years, and a thousand years as one day." On that basis, assuming we lived to one hundred, to Naomi it would be as if we were gone for an hour and a half!

A fresh perspective lifted our spirits. Notice the verse in 2 Peter 3:8 starts with the words: *"do not forget this one thing..."* When everything going on down here seems senseless, we need to get a heavenly perspective. It will all be over very shortly. We have one shot at life so let's give it our best. Proverbs 24:16 (NIV) says, "For though the righteous fall seven times, they rise again..." Any time the devil knocks you down, get back up knowing the time is short.

## GLOBAL PERSPECTIVE

During this same season in our lives, my husband and I were watching the news. At the time, there were devastating floods in Mozambique. We saw footage of a father who had walked eighteen miles with his two year old daughter in his arms. He and his family had been without fresh water for days and the situation had become desperate.

Journalists found this man just as he reached water. While the cameras were still rolling, this man realized that his daughter had passed away moments beforehand. Sitting in a warm home, we knew that there were thousands facing far greater hardship than we would ever know. There was something about that catastrophe which put our own tragedy into context. A different perspective helped us to count our blessings.

# SMALL FRY

Paul the apostle suffered way more than most. He was beaten, stoned, imprisoned and ship-wrecked. He went without food and endured sleepless nights. He described his experiences in 2 Corinthians 4:8-9, 11a, 17 (NLT): "We are pressed on every side by troubles, but we are not crushed. We are perplexed, but not driven to despair. We are hunted down, but never abandoned by God. We get knocked down, but we are not destroyed... Yes, we live under constant danger of death... Though our bodies are dying, our spirits are being renewed every day. For our present troubles are small and won't last very long. Yet they produce for us a glory that vastly outweighs them and will last forever!"

Each time Paul mentioned a difficulty, he included a caveat which put his problem into perspective. It reduced the drama. Then in verse 17 of the above passage, the apostle wrote: "... our present troubles are small and won't last very long..." Paul described his physical and emotional anguish as small trials. He refused to see his suffering as a big deal and instead focused on the fruit that his pain produced. He chose an outlook that helped him endure with a positive attitude.

Colossians 3:1-2 (MSG) is powerful: "So if you're serious about living this new resurrection life with Christ, act like it. Pursue the things over which Christ presides. Don't shuffle along, eyes to the ground, absorbed with the things right in front of you. Look up, and be alert to what is going on around Christ—that's where the action is. See things from his perspective." Let's lift up our eyes and see things the way the Lord does.

# TAKING ACTION

The Psalmist understood the necessity of taking his eyes off his circumstances and focusing on his Heavenly Father: "I lift my eyes to you, O God, enthroned in heaven. We keep looking to the Lord our God for His mercy, just as servants keep their eyes on their master, as a slave girl watches her mistress for the slightest signal." (Psalm 123:1-2 NLT) When times are tough, it always helps when we put our eyes on the Lord. I do not mean that we should tell Him how woeful our lives have been! I mean we need to worship and praise. The psalmist was focusing on the majesty and mercy of our God. You can pick one of God's attributes and just think about that for a while.

Self-centered thinking needs to be corrected. 2 Corinthians 10:6 shows us how: "...Bringing every thought into captivity..." We need to make a decision not to tolerate inner conversations that have self at the center. There is always someone who needs our attention, our love, our concern. Why don't you determine that you will deal with all self-absorption? We live in a big world with a multitude of problems and we can be part of the solution. When we shift our attention, we become more useful to the kingdom. Romans 12:2b says, "Let God transform you into a new person by changing the way you think." Removing self-centeredness from our thinking will be liberating and life-changing. Let's pray:

**Heavenly Father,**

I am so grateful for Your mercy and patience with me. I am sorry for seeing my issues towering above the suffering of others. I realize that there are people all around me who have gone through similar pain and many who have faced far greater difficulties. I have had a self-absorbed outlook on life so I ask for Your forgiveness. My lot in life is not worse and my pain does not make me different. Please give me new love and compassion for other people.

I am sorry for every sense of entitlement that I have held. I thought my suffering gave me special rights, but I was wrong. Please forgive me and help me to be grateful for every good gift that You have given me. Help me to see every day of my life as a heaven-sent opportunity.

I take responsibility today for the state of my life and for my choices. Forgive me for blaming others for my circumstances. I take back control of my future by accepting responsibility for my actions and my attitudes. I choose an optimistic outlook on my life. I choose to be grateful.

Thank you, Lord, that the troubles I have experienced are small and will pass soon. My suffering is preparing me for my destiny and it is making me more mature. I am so glad that You are the Lord of all. You are on Your throne and today is a very good day!

I give You all the praise and glory, in Jesus' name,

Amen.

# Chapter 10

# PRAISE

My parents had been married for 55 years when my father passed away. After a lifetime of companionship, my mother was alone for the first time. Four days after my father died, I asked my mother how she was doing. I will never forget her reply: "The spirit of heaviness tries to come on me, but I push it away. I use the Word and I praise. That's what Christians do, isn't it?" I was stunned. I responded, "Mum, that's amazing. I'm sure that is what we are *supposed* to do, but I'm not sure many would actually manage to do that in your position."

My mother grieved the death of my father and she poured out her pain in His presence. At the same time, she made praise a weapon to fight off despondency. She refused to allow heaviness to settle in her heart and instead regularly reminded herself of the goodness of God. She worked hard to keep herself from self-pity. As a result, she came out the other side strong.

## GRUMBLING

Although we do not live under the Old Covenant, the Old Testament can give us great insight into the heart of God: "Soon the people began to complain about their hardship, and the Lord heard everything they said. Then the Lord's anger blazed against them, and he sent a fire to rage among them, and he destroyed some of the people in the outskirts of the camp." Numbers 11:1 (NLT). The Israelites were not grumbling on the mountaintop. That would be very ungrateful. They were complaining about their hardships.

It cannot have been easy to walk through the wilderness in soaring temperatures without a permanent resting place. There were young families, pregnant ladies, nursing mothers and very old people. They all had to walk, day after day. If you are anything like me, you probably enjoy a variety of food. They had to eat the same meals every day for years! Despite the difficulty of their circumstances, God saw their grumbling as an appalling display of ingratitude.

Thank God for the cross. We live in the era of God's mercy, which means nobody is going to die today for complaining! However, we can hear God's heart on the matter: it grieves Him when we grumble. Although He will never leave us, the Holy Spirit will be kept at bay by our murmuring. In truth, it hurts us too. When we whine, it saps our energy and weighs us down. Words either bring death or breathe life (Proverbs 18:21). Negativity paves the way for discontentment and discouragement. It not only brings us down, but it affects the people around us too. No one really wants to be around a moaner.

A few years ago, I brought one of my leaders on a ministry trip. We stayed in various places as I was ministering in different churches and conferences. Unfortunately, nothing seemed to be quite right for my travel companion. The first day, the breakfast was not up to scratch. That night, the air conditioning was not strong enough. When we went to the next hotel, it was too cold. It was exhausting! This woman loved God with all her heart so I knew that once she saw her shortcomings, she would deal with her heart. We had a chat about the antidote and this woman became grateful. It not only changed her life, it made her a joy to be around.

## CHOOSING TO REMEMBER

We all know people who have it all and yet seem dissatisfied. On the other hand, it is humbling to meet those who are always overflowing with joy despite life's difficulties. After God delivered the children of Israel from the Egyptians, He instructed them to instigate an annual feast. And what was the purpose of this party? 'This annual festival will be a visible sign to you, like a mark branded on your hand or your forehead. Let the festival remind you always to recite... "With a strong hand, the Lord delivered you from Egypt."' Ex 13:9. God established an annual convention for one reason alone: so that His people would never forget His goodness. It was so important that they remembered God's deliverance that He created a public holiday.

So how does that apply to you and me? How many times do we pray for something to happen, or not to happen? When God comes through, we may say thank you but soon forget His kindness. When we turn a corner and times are tough again, we quickly complain. The Lord wants us to make every effort to remember His goodness. When you face a trial, think back to your last testimony. When life is tough, remind yourself that God is good.

Several years ago, my husband ministered in the nation of Mozambique. It is one of the poorest countries in the world where men, women and children experience hardship that would be hard for most of us in the west to even imagine. As my husband arrived at a conference there, a local choir was singing songs of thanksgiving. It lit up the night with radiant joy. Members sang for more than an hour in the cold and rain. My husband was moved beyond measure as he tried to imagine the slum homes that many of those precious people would return to afterwards. They obviously weren't thankful because of their circumstances. They were thankful in spite of their circumstances.

Gratitude isn't just a healthy suggestion to improve our lives. It is God's will for you and me. 1 Thessalonians 5:18 (AMPC) says, "Thank [God] in everything [no matter what the circumstances may be, be thankful and give thanks], for this is the will of God for you [who are] in Christ Jesus..." Whatever we are experiencing, there is always something for which we can be thankful. It is a choice to obey one of the Lord's commandments. It is not always easy, but it is always possible.

# BLOCKERS

As 2019 drew to a close, I knew my attitude towards 2020 had to change. Proverbs 23:18 (KJV) says that our: "... expectation shall not be cut off." Put simply, that means that we get what we expect. Every time I looked to 2020, I was heavy-hearted. I felt like I could not handle another hard year. God took me on a remarkable journey...

First, I did what I knew I should do. I went to the Lord and told Him about every disappointment in the year that had been. We had encountered financial challenges. Also, although the transformational anointing at all our events was phenomenal, attendance in certain regions was low. I poured out every sadness in my soul and gave it all to Him. Leaving my prayer closet, I was much lighter and could look forward with more faith.

However, something was still stuck. My heart was not fully free to believe the best for 2020. When I looked back at 2019, I still found myself feeling sad. I prayed again using Rebekah's Request in Genesis 25:22b: "If all is well, why am I like this?" The Lord took me back to one particular event. I realized that whenever I thought of 2019, I saw this meeting. I asked the Lord what it was about this event that weighed me down. Almost immediately, He revealed an argument hidden in my heart. He showed me ten empty rooms. An underground river of disappointment and confusion burst through to the surface.

Let me explain. When I book events, I have to estimate how many people will attend. I attempt to use a mixture of faith and wisdom to agree numbers and sign contracts. For the first five years of our ministry, each event was near enough to contract. However, 2019 was different. I overestimated numbers several times. At one particular event, we had ten empty rooms that could have accommodated up to 30 people. The financial implications are obvious and had caused me great concern. But it was not just that. Those ten empty rooms were talking to me. Obstacles can do that, you know...

## LOOK WHAT'S TALKING

Do you remember the story of Jesus cursing a fig tree? Mark 11:13-14 (KJV) says, 'And seeing a fig tree afar off having leaves, he came, if he might find any thing thereon: and when he came to it, he found nothing but leaves.. And *Jesus answered and said unto it*, "No man eat fruit of thee hereafter for ever."' I have italicized the words I want you to notice. If Jesus answered the fig tree, it must have been talking to Him. Of course, I know that trees can't speak English - or any other known language for that matter! Nonetheless, this fig tree was saying something to Jesus. It provoked our Lord and Savior and He spoke back and silenced the provocation. Maybe something from your past is speaking to you. Perhaps a mistake you made many years ago is telling you that you won't succeed if you try again.

Those ten empty rooms were telling me that I could not be trusted to sign contracts. They were telling me that I had missed the mark. They were making me feel like a failure. They were an inner argument that wouldn't go away. I wept before the Lord and asked Him what I should do. I heard Him say, "Give the empty rooms to me." At first I did not want to. It felt like giving in or ignoring the facts. However, I relented and handed them over to the Lord. As soon as I said amen, the load on my shoulders lifted. I felt free!

# THE REAL GAME-CHANGER

The weight of the year was gone. However, I still felt somewhat deflated about 2020 so I asked the Lord what I should do next. I knew I had to enter the New Year full of faith and expectation. God then led me to review the previous year from start to finish with one goal in mind: gratitude. I sat in the presence of the Lord and starting in January, I thanked God for every good gift. I was amazed at how many wonderful things the Lord had done! Life-changing events full to overflowing with His precious healing anointing, unexpected generous donations, old friends, new friends, family vacations, miracles and breakthroughs.

Within minutes (and I mean minutes), all the heaviness was gone and I was in awe of the goodness of God. By the time I had made my way to December, I was blown away by what a glorious year I had just enjoyed. My heart was now full of faith for 2020. The same God who was faithful in 2019 would do more than I could ask or imagine in 2020! Praise transformed my perspective and made me ready for the year ahead.

Philippians 4:6 says, "Be anxious for nothing, but in everything by prayer and supplication, with thanksgiving, let your requests be made known to God." The right way to take tablets is with water. You could swallow pills without liquid, but they might get stuck in your throat. Similarly, the right way to pray about our needs and desires is *with* thanksgiving. We can use a petition on its own, but our prayers may get stuck. Gratitude turbocharges our time with God. By focusing our attention on the faithfulness of our Heavenly Father, it builds our faith for Him to do it again. Thanksgiving in prayer needs to become a way of life. Not only is it God's will, it keeps our pretend friend away. Just as insect sprays keep mosquitoes away, so gratitude repels self-pity.

# DOOR-OPENER

One of the first verses I learnt as a child was Psalm 100:4: "Enter His gates with thanksgiving and His courts with praise." I can only conclude: "No thanksgiving? No entry." The most powerful place in existence is out of bounds to me if my heart isn't thankful. The place where every answer is made plain has restricted access. Only the thankful get through the gates. Gratitude is a door-opener. The Message puts this verse beautifully: 'Enter with the password: "Thank you!"'

Let thanksgiving become your passport to your next breakthrough. Complaining is quickly dispelled by the joy from thanksgiving. If you are from a nation, region or family with a propensity to whine, you will have to purpose in your heart that you will not go the way of your predecessors. Thanksgiving is a powerful tool to transform the very atmosphere of our lives. Based on Psalm 100:4 and Philippians 4:6 alone, I believe that a gratitude deficit can keep us out of God's best for our lives.

Luke 17:11-19 tells the story of when Jesus cleansed ten lepers. However, only one returned to give glory to God. Jesus was clearly saddened that nine men neglected to thank Him. It is interesting that after the one returned to show his appreciation, Jesus said these words: "Arise, go your way. Your faith has made you well." (Luke 17:19). At the start of this story, Jesus cleansed ten lepers, but thanksgiving released a greater miracle for the one. He was made well. The Greek word for well is sōzō and it encapsulates the idea of complete salvation and total wellbeing. It means to be made whole. Gratitude granted this man a ticket to a better life.

## LIFESTYLE

Most Bibles end Colossians 3:15 with the words, "... and be thankful." Young's Literal Translation (YLT) puts it differently. It says: "... and become thankful." Scripture is calling us to a lifestyle of thanksgiving, not just a moment of gratitude. A spiritual daughter who struggled her whole life with this issue once asked me, "So what does the opposite of self-pity look like?" It looks like a life overflowing with thankfulness.

In Britain, we punctuate our days with tea! We wake up and have a cup of tea. Some bad news arrives so we have a cup of tea. We get a breakthrough so (yes you've guessed it) we have a cup of tea! Imagine what your life would feel like if you punctuated your day with gratitude. You wake up in the morning and start your day by thanking God for His faithfulness. As you're standing in line at the grocery store, you're giving God glory. When there is no time for lunch, you're expressing gratitude that you have a job.

Colossians 3:17 goes on to say, "And whatever you do in word or deed, do all in the name of the Lord Jesus, giving thanks to God the Father through Him." In other words, this verse is encouraging us to be thanking the Lord whatever we are doing or saying. We need to thank God that we woke up, and then thank Him that we have hot water for a shower. We need to be grateful for the food on our plate and appreciative of the roof over our heads. We need to rejoice when it rains, as well as when the sun shines. Whatever we do, we need to be giving thanks to God in our hearts. We will be so busy praising, we won't have time for self-pity!

# KICKING OUT DISCOURAGEMENT

Isaac found a way of fighting discouragement. As he attempted to secure a source of drinking water for himself and his family, his efforts were thwarted again and again (see Genesis 26:18-22). Every time he broke through and dug a new well, the enemy took over. It would have been very easy for Isaac to feel defeated. Instead, he rose up, moved on and started again. He refused to allow failure and disappointment to keep him down. Sometimes we need a little help to get to where Isaac was. The sludge of life can somehow block the well of joy that God wants to give us.

When we rejoice, it releases joy deep within. The joy of the Lord is our strength and when we rejoice, we release the inner strength to rise above our circumstances. The name Isaac means laughter. I believe he learned to laugh at a very young age so he knew what to do as an adult when things got tough! Proverbs 17:22 teaches us that a merry heart does us good, just like medicine. I can be very serious so I am glad that God gave me a witty husband, a hilarious spiritual mother and a wonderfully funny covenant friend. Laughter does you good. Find someone who can help you let it out. I'm not very funny, but thankfully they make up for it. Let's learn from Isaac and laugh at the obstacles of life.

# THE BEST WAY

We have learned a lot about self-pity. Our pretend friend feels sorry for itself, it is dissatisfied with life, it feels badly done by and it moans. The opposite of feeling sorry for yourself is counting your blessings. The opposite of dissatisfaction is contentment. The opposite of feeling badly done by is being grateful. The opposite of moaning is praising. The opposite of self-pity is rejoicing!

Inspired by the Holy Spirit, Paul the apostle instructed Christians to rejoice - ALL THE TIME! (Philippians 4:4). This verse charges us to be joyful when life is tough. Paul clearly practiced what he preached. Despite terrible suffering, Paul's letters were full of thanksgiving and praise. This man would not allow circumstances to steal his joy. If anyone had the right to feel sorry for himself, it was Paul. Yet this mighty man always chose to rejoice. The Greek for rejoice is chairō and it means to be cheerful, happy, to be joyful and to be glad. Rejoicing is a choice and it is one that you and I need to make again and again and again!

## NOTHING TO DO WITH CIRCUMSTANCES

Paul described some of his trials in 2 Corinthians 11:24-27 (NLT): "Five different times the Jewish leaders gave me thirty-nine lashes. Three times I was beaten with rods. Once I was stoned. Three times I was shipwrecked. Once I spent a whole night and a day adrift at sea. I have traveled on many long journeys. I have faced danger from rivers and from robbers. I have faced danger from my own people, the Jews, as well as from the Gentiles. I have faced danger in the cities, in the deserts, and on the seas. And I have faced danger from men who claim to be believers but are not. I have worked hard and long, enduring many sleepless nights. I have been hungry and thirsty and have often gone without food. I have shivered in the cold, without enough clothing to keep me warm."

I haven't gone through a fraction of this man's anguish. His suffering probably makes your trials seem insignificant as well. Even if you think you have encountered greater trouble, Scripture still says, "Rejoice in the Lord always [delight, gladden yourselves in Him]; again I say, Rejoice!" (Philippians 4:4 AMPC). Why did the Holy Spirit feel the need to repeat Himself in the same verse? Because He knew that you and I would need to have this lesson drilled into our hearts and minds. We are called to be glad in every season. We are instructed to rejoice whatever we are facing. When we obey, we send our pretend friend packing.

## DELIBERATELY DISMANTLING EXCUSES

There are times when I have felt sorry for myself simply because my train was delayed or a friend let me down. In contrast, Paul the apostle endured hunger and beatings without batting an eyelid. He deliberately dismantled his excuses for self-pity. This amazing man wrote four New Testament letters from jail and exuded joy through the pages. It is all too easy to see praise as something we should do when things go well. Of course, we should give God all the glory on the mountaintop. However, praise is even more powerful when it is a sacrifice offered from the valleys of our lives.

Praise is a game-changer. It confuses the enemy, shuts down his accusations and gives us supernatural strength. Psalms 8:2 says, "Out of the mouth of babes and nursing infants You have ordained strength, because of Your enemies, that You may silence the enemy and the avenger." The Hebrew word here for strength is ôz and it means praise or majesty. The fact that the same word means strength and praise says so much.

When we praise, we become strong. Strength arises inside when we boldly declare the majesty of God. Our praise does not just build us up, it also shuts satan down. The end of this verse explains that even when children praise, the enemy is silenced. I don't know about you, but I have had enough of the devil's lies. Let's shut him up with our praises.

# TURNAROUND

There are many scriptural examples of how praise turned people's lives around. One of my favorites involves our beloved apostle Paul. We will pick up the story in Acts 16:22-24 (NLT): "A mob quickly formed against Paul and Silas, and the city officials ordered them to be stripped and beaten with wooden rods. They were severely beaten, and then they were thrown into prison. The jailer was ordered to make sure they didn't escape. So the jailer put them into the inner dungeon and clamped their feet in the stocks."

Paul and Silas must have been in agony after the brutal beating. Now they were locked up with their ankles clamped in irons. These dungeons were dark, damp and dirty. Their flesh must have felt like crying or complaining. Instead, these men of God took their eyes off their circumstances and gave God praise: "Around midnight Paul and Silas were praying and singing hymns to God, and the other prisoners were listening." (Acts 16:25 NLT).

# RELEASING POWER

Right now, why don't you stop and pray for a moment? Ask the Holy Spirit to remind you of this story next time you are facing a distressing situation. If Paul praised when he was in pain in prison, you and I can do the same when we are suffering. Rejoicing in the middle of storms actually enables us to endure otherwise unbearable situations. It gives us strength.

There is a famous verse that says, "...the joy of the Lord is your strength" (Nehemiah 8:10b). You and I desperately need an injection of supernatural strength when we are struggling. So how do we get the joy we need to become strong? We get it by rejoicing - which at its simplest means practicing joy! Praise produces joy and joy releases strength. That alone would be enough reason to praise all the time, but it does not stop there...

While Paul and Silas were singing songs to God, the Holy Spirit was planning their escape: "Suddenly, there was a massive earthquake, and the prison was shaken to its foundations. All the doors immediately flew open, and the chains of every prisoner fell off!" (Acts 16:26 NLT). Praise provoked a powerful move of God's Spirit, a breakthrough in their circumstances and the salvation of a household. If you will praise when all hell is breaking loose in your life, you may find that all heaven breaks loose on your behalf instead.

The difficulty of our everyday situations can all too easily drown out any feeling of thanksgiving. The list of griefs and sorrows we bear can be very long. Our challenge is to make the right choices even in the midst of every painful trial. We need to kick out our pretend friend and instead embrace the abundant life Jesus died to provide (John 10:10). Remember, gratitude opens the door to the manifest presence of God and praise generates joy and strength. You will be amazed how much happier life is when you practice praise on a daily basis. Let's pray:

**Heavenly Father,**

I realize that I have withheld praise and thanksgiving far too many times. Please forgive me for feeling sorry for myself when I should have been counting my blessings. I am sorry for moaning when I should have been praising. There are times when I have accommodated self-pity when I should have been rejoicing. Forgive me Lord.

Today I choose to rejoice. I choose to be grateful. I choose to be glad. I decide to remember every good thing You have done for me. Help me, Lord, to create new habits of gratitude. I decide to become a praiser. I will declare your goodness when all is well, but I will also rejoice when life is tough. Help me to correct any praise deficit in my life. Thank You, Lord, for heaven's remedies to self-pity. I will kick my foul pretend friend out of my life once and for all and I will become victorious.

I give You all the praise and glory for all You have done!

In Jesus' name,

Amen.

# WHAT NEXT?

Your heart is probably your most valuable, and yet your most vulnerable, asset. This book is just part of your journey to wholeness and freedom. As you finish this book, make the decision to continue to prioritize your inner wellbeing. Visit our website JoNaughton.com to find out about our range of resources to help you to wholeness. We have online courses and a range of print, digital and audio books. We run half day, full day and two-day events all designed to help you on your journey. Above all, look after your heart every day of your life for it determines the course of your life.

"I am convinced and sure of this very thing, that He Who began a good work in you will continue until the day of Jesus Christ (right up to the time of His return), developing [that good work] and perfecting and bringing it to full completion in you." (Philippians 1:6 AMP)

Let that word sink deep into you. God is preparing you for your destiny. He has already started the job and He will be faithful to finish it.

# AN INVITATION

If you would like to ask Jesus to become the Lord of your life, I would be honored to lead you in a simple prayer. The Bible says that God loves you and that Jesus wants to draw close to you: "Behold I stand at the door and knock. If anyone hears My voice and opens the door, I will come in." (Revelation 3:20). If you would like to know Jesus as your Friend, your Savior and your Lord, the first step is to ask. Pray this prayer:

Dear Lord,

I know that You love me and have a wonderful plan for my life. I ask You to come into my heart today and be my Savior and Lord. Forgive me for all my sins, I pray. Thank You that because You died on the cross for me, I am forgiven of every wrong I have ever committed when I repent. I give my life to You entirely and ask You to lead me in Your ways from now on.

In Jesus' name,

Amen.

If you have prayed this prayer for the first time, it will be important to tell a Christian friend what you prayed and to find a good church. Just as a newborn baby needs nourishment and care, so you (and all Christians) need the support of other believers as you start your new life as a follower of Jesus Christ.

You can watch free Bible messages that will help to build your faith on Harvest Church London's YouTube channel. You can follow me on Instagram (@naughtonjo), go on Facebook and like my public page (Jo Naughton), subscribe to my YouTube channel (Jo Naughton) and follow me on Twitter (@naughtonjo). God bless you!

# ABOUT THE AUTHOR

Jo Naughton is the founder of Healed for Life, a ministry dedicated to helping people be free to fulfill their God-given purpose. Together with her husband Paul, Jo pastors Harvest Church in London, England. A public relations executive turned pastor, Jo's previous career included working for Prince Charles as an executive VP of his largest charity. After reaching the pinnacle of the public relations world, Jo felt the call of God to full-time ministry. She is a regular guest on TV and radio shows in the US and UK.

An international speaker and author, Jo ministers with a heart-piercing anointing, sharing with great personal honesty in conferences and at churches around the world. Her passion is to see people set free from all inner hindrances so that they can fulfill their God-given destiny. Countless people have testified to having received powerful and life-changing healing through her ministry. Jo and Paul have two wonderful children, Ben and Abby.

You can connect with Jo via:
JoNaughton.com
Instagram (@naughtonjo)
YouTube (Jo Naughton)
Facebook (public page - Jo Naughton)
Twitter (@naughtonjo)
For more information about Harvest Church London, visit harvestchurch.org.uk

# Also by the Author:

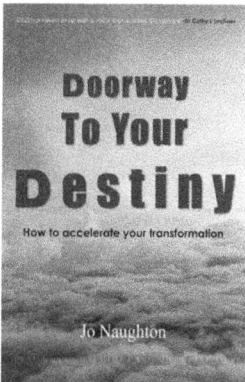

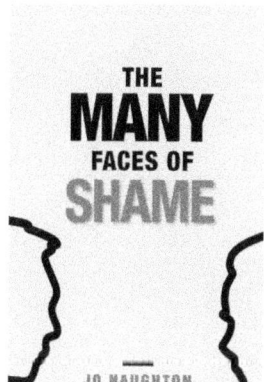

All Jo Naughton's books are available at: JoNaughton.com